the
Serpent
and the
Dove

What Scripture teaches us about the world,
who we are, and the wonder of being alive

Robert W Cely

The Serpent and the Dove

What Scripture teaches us
about the world,
who we are,
and the wonder of being alive.

The Serpent and the Dove
By Robert W Cely

ISBN 978-1-64594-051-7

Published by Athanatos Publishing Group.

Introduction:

Finding Hope in a Hopeless Word

I write this introduction from the middle point of the year 2020. At this time, the world, and especially America, is experiencing unprecedented turmoil. We are at the end of a long shutdown of social and economic activity due to the COVID-19 outbreak, one that will have far-reaching consequences. Riots have flared up in cities across the country, beginning with protests against police violence, and ending with more violence than what was initially protested. To top it all off, the political climate is one of deep divide, partisanship, hostility, and mistrust.

This is a crisis, I believe, that has been brewing for some time. I also believe that this is not the peak of the crisis. This is just one outburst, one overflow of the problems that are stirring beneath the surface. More than likely, this will settle down and life will resume some of its normalcy. But it isn't going away. Pressure will continue to build, more outbursts to follow. These will continue until we either address the root of the problem, or they weaken the system and a final outburst brings chaos down on our heads.

Most people will look at these problems and crises as political, economic or social issues. They will claim it is the racist system, inherent inequalities, a rigged political process, or simply the wrong party in place at the present time. The solution, therefore, is to make the right systematic or political changes and the sinking ship will right itself. This is an incredibly naive and shortsighted way to look at our issues. Were we to change those things mentioned above, we would only address the symptoms, not the problem.

What I see occurring is that the West, and most of its

people, are in the midst of a great existential crisis, despite the fact that most do not know they are in this crisis, or even understand what an existential crisis is.

An existential crisis is when a person is taken over by the thought or feeling that life has no real purpose or meaning. Life is pointless. Life is worthless. Life is empty. Nothing matters. These are the trademark emotions of a person in the throes of such a turmoil.

This is where I see us as a people. We are, collectively, and individually, in the midst of a crisis of meaning and purpose. We have lost a sense of purpose, and so we have lost direction in life. With a lost sense of purpose, we have also lost any sense of identity. We can't really say who we are, or what our place is in society or the larger context of the world. There is no truth that we can cling to, for even the idea of truth has been thrown away. Reason and thought suffer. Our ideological foundations have become porous and soft, unable to hold us up any longer.

Most notably and consequentially, we have lost hope. This is the greatest and deepest symptom of the existential crisis, a loss of hope. We no longer look forward to the future. Our image of tomorrow is grim and dark, full of ecological disaster, economic ruin, and social isolation. Without hope, we struggle to work for the benefit of the future, resigning ourselves to the pleasures of the day. We don't look forward to what tomorrow may bring but look forward with dread. This is the most damaging feature of our crisis.

Many writers and poets, visionaries and social thinkers have watched this crisis looming, and warned the West for a long time. As such, many books have been written about the problems that confront our culture. This is not one of those books. Rather, this is one about solutions.

I believe that if we were to trace our crisis to its very root, we would find an idea. That is the heart of our

2

dilemma, an idea. Or rather, it is several ideas. These are very important ideas, for they form the foundations of our religious, ethical and philosophical outlooks. These ideas form our worldview. They answer such essential questions as: How did we get here? Why were we created? How was the universe made? What is the nature of humanity? What is the origin of evil? What can we do about evil? How should we live? What is our purpose?

These are fundamental questions, fundamental ideas. Every culture has answers to them, as does every person. Even if we do not think about them, in unconscious ways we carry answers to these questions with us in everything we do. They inform our culture, our art, our science, education, politics, law, everything. They form the basis, the root ideas, from which all our other ideas concerning life spring forth.

Today, these essential questions are answered with a materialist outlook on life. Even if you do not agree with materialism, our culture abides by the ideas of a materialistic philosophy and outlook. And this outlook has very specific answers to the fundamental questions mentioned above.

How did we get here? We got here by accident, by a long series of cause and effect beginning with an explosion known as the Big Bang.

Why were we created? For no particular reason. It just happened, like everything else.

How was the universe made? It was made by the inevitable collusion of force and matter, dictated by the laws of the universe.

What is the nature of humanity? Man is an animal, albeit a clever one. He is a bipedal mammal with a large brain.

What is the origin of evil? This is a nonsense question, as evil is an outdated construct from an older world. There is no evil. There are only people making bad choices. People make bad choices because of brain chemistry, poor upbringing, or economic inequality.

What can we do about evil? We prevent children from making bad choices by giving them everything they want and striving our hardest to make sure they do not experience even the briefest moment of suffering. We hope to persuade adult people to make better choices through massive social welfare programs to correct economic inequality.

How should we live? In whatever way makes us happy.

What is our purpose? There is no purpose to life. Our purpose is what we make it to be. This is especially true with societies. We have no collective purpose except to provide the individual with the things he wants that will make him happy.

These are the implications of materialism. If the world is made only of matter, if there is no supreme being or deity that transcends the world, then theses conclusions are inevitable. Despite the objections of the materialists to the contrary, if you were to peel back their arguments far enough, or force them into a straight answer to your questions, this is where you would arrive. Life has no purpose.

Because these are the implications of the ideas that our culture assumes, it should come as no surprise that we are engaged in an existential crisis. It should come as no surprise we struggle to find purpose and meaning. It should come as no surprise we feel alienated and apathetic. It should come as no surprise that we have lost hope.

It is important to note that these ideas, and even the existential crisis it causes, are not necessarily the cause of our problems. Problems have various causes in life, and will always be with us. This we have to accept.

4

What is deeply troubling about our crisis, about this crisis of ideas, is that it undermines our ability to confront and solve the problems that face us today. We even fail to identify some very glaring issues as problems at all. Without the right ideas forming our view of life, we will have great difficulties distinguishing between good and evil, regarding properly what is harmful from helpful, identifying truth from lies, and even recognizing when life has jumped the proverbial track and plunges headlong into oblivion.

As I noted before, there have been many books written about these problems. I do not attempt to rehash work that has been done often, and better, than I could do. This, instead, is a book about solutions.

This is a book about ideas. These are ideas about life, humanity, the nature of the universe, and the purpose of life. This is about fundamental ideas that should form the basis of all of our views about who we are and why we are here. This is a book about the most essential questions that we can, and should, ask.

I do not deceive myself so much as to think that I could discover or formulate these ideas all on my own. I cannot. These questions are much too big for me to tackle. All I can do is stand on the shoulders of giants and repeat to you what they have taught me.

This is why I have turned to the Bible for my answers. It is the inspired word of God, given to mankind for his instruction. It is the final authority in matters of faith.

I do, however, realize that not everyone feels the same way about scripture as I do. To them, the Bible may be, at best, an antiquated collection of stories told by superstitious people. At worst, it is a mythology of hatred and cruelty that has been used for systematic oppression the world over.

For the total haters of the Bible, I have little to say. In

fact, if you feel that way, it is best you do not waste another moment of your time and put this book down right now. You will very likely remain unconvinced by anything I have to say. Moreover, you have already closed your mind off and decided what is true (if truth even exists), so nothing can penetrate the armor of your intellectual dogma.

But for the others, even if you do believe that the Bible is nothing more than stories, I would argue that old stories have much to teach us. And of all old stories, mythology can teach us the most. It is one of the greatest tragedies of modern language that myth has become a word synonymous with lie. It is a tragedy and an irony, for myth contains much truth. In fact, myth contains more truth than you will find in scientific journals, for they confine themselves to fact. And fact, contrary to popular usage, is not the opposite of myth. In defending this idea of mythology, I will defer to the works of men like CG Jung and Joseph Campbell.

If we turn to the Bible, to the first book, called Genesis, to the first few chapters, we will find a fascinating story. It is the story of the creation of the cosmos. It is the story of the creation of humanity. It tells us how this all got started and why. It tells us how humanity, after being created, fell, and evil infiltrated the world. More importantly, it tells us how evil can be overcome.

The story of Genesis is the story of what it means to be alive. It gives a very different answer than the one our culture gives us about how and why we got here. If it is a myth, it is one so full of truth that we should reclaim that word from error.

Genesis tells us a very important story. Some would say it is the most important story, so it is necessary that we reclaim it. For it is in this story, not the one our culture teaches and assumes as true, that we discover the truth of who we are. It is this truth, and this truth alone, that has the ability to set us free from the despair that overwhelms us today.

With the right ideas, we can emerge from the existential crisis that has gripped our nation and all of Western civilization. With the right story we can reclaim a sense of purpose and passion for life that seems to be lost to us today. With the right story, we can reclaim hope.

Of all ideas about life, this is the greatest one that the story of Genesis gives us—it gives us hope. And hope is in desperate need for our world at this hour.

Hope is what keeps us looking forward to the future. Hope believes tomorrow can be bright. When we believe that, believe in a good future, it enables us to work for the future, to build a better tomorrow, to build a better world for our children, instead of ransoming their futures for today's quick solution. If we are to find our way out of this crisis, it is by reclaiming a hope in tomorrow.

To do this, we need to find our hope again. We need to be people of hope. We need to rediscover a future that we can work towards and believe in. And if we are to do those things, we have to first live in a universe that can offer hope. We have to be people who were created with a reason to hope.

If we look to our current mythology of the universe and human origins, we find little reason to hope at all. In that story, we are surrounded by a dark and cold universe in which we exist as inconsequential specks that are not even noticed by the endless expanse of space.

If we are to find hope, we must peer deeper. We must refer to older stories, perhaps less sophisticated, but more wise by far. We must look to one of the first stories ever told about how we got here and why. It is there that we will find the secret of being human, the secret of being alive, and the secret to our future.

Part I

–

The Creation of the World

1 - Genesis 1:1-2

In the Beginning

In the beginning, God created the heavens and the earth. The earth was without form and void, and darkness was over the face of the deep. And the Spirit of God was hovering over the face of the waters.

In the beginning.

This is how it begins. In the beginning.

People like to ask "What happened before the beginning?" They ask as if it is a legitimate inquiry for human beings to make. The truth is, we do not know what happened before the beginning. And even worse, we cannot know. We likely will never know.

What happened before everything got started?

The answer is, nothing.

Nothing happened before the beginning. Nothing **can** happen before the beginning. That is what the beginning means. This is the moment when everything started. Nothing happened before this moment, because, before this moment, nothing had happened.

We don't like to accept this answer. Our modern pursuit of information has trained us to disassemble, dissect and take apart so that we may understand the mechanisms behind all things. We want to know what happened before something happened, because if we know that, then we can better understand the cause of what happened.

So, we ask ourselves, what happened before the beginning? If we know what happened before the beginning, then we can finally understand the nature of reality. We can understand and know the true power that lies in all things and through all things. And in knowing, we gain ultimate mastery over this world.

But we cannot know what happened before the beginning.

You see, the beginning of the world, the beginning of creation, is also the beginning of our knowledge. This is as far back as it can stretch. The human mind can only perceive so far back in time. It is a mind of cause and effect, and we strive to understand everything in terms of cause and effect. But, when we look back past the beginning, past the moment when there was no effect, we come up empty. Our minds go blank and they grasp at nothing. For this is the beginning. This is as far back as we can go.

This is a basic truth that every human being must accept about life: there are clear limits to human understanding. There is a barrier that each of us will come up against as we strive to understand our world. For some, that limit of knowledge is very distant - wise and intelligent men among us who understand far more than the average person. There are those whose limit is a very short one, who understand far less. But we all have that limit. No matter how brilliant or dull a person may be, his knowledge and understanding can go no further than this boundary: in the beginning.

The idea may be frustrating to many, and many still deny this limit. But it is there all the same. The intelligent have a harder time with this concept than the average man. As a consequence, they struggle against it and refuse to accept it. A mind that can understand most things bristles at the idea that there may be something he doesn't understand. The idea even comes with a touch of fear. Those who understand much are the most afraid of that which they do not understand.

This is not just a quaint little point to make in order to humble those who pretend to know it all or to bring down those materialists who insist on the ultimate triumph of human knowledge that is more intelligent than matter. This is a fact of life.

Not only is it a fact of human existence, it is a key part of the human condition. It is necessary to understand and accept this if we are ever to understand what life is all about. This is even more important to accept if we are to ever recover the thrill of being alive.

The quickest way to take the joy out of living is to place oneself in the position of God. Those who insist on knowing everything, understanding everything, and worst of all, controlling everything, are the most miserable people among us. For them, life has lost its luster. The more we insist on control and understanding, the more miserable we become.

That is not to say that knowledge is bad. Knowledge is good. Knowledge and understanding are very good, one of the best things that a man can pursue.

It is not knowledge and understanding that make us miserable. It is the insistence that we understand everything that makes us miserable. That is where we begin to take the joy out of life and make it a burden and a misery.

To accept the limits of our knowledge, accept that there are mysteries out there we will never understand, is to begin to be enchanted once again with life. We all must accept our limits. And we all have them. One of these is the limit of "in the beginning."

In the beginning.

This is where it starts for us. We know that a thing cannot create itself. Nothing makes itself. All things have to be made by something that preceded it. Our universe could not have made itself.

This is self-evident. Nothing can create itself. So, if the universe could not have made itself, then something or someone had to create it.

Here we reach the limits of our understanding. Who could create himself? Who could be when there was yet any being?

We can never know this. The start of all the cause and effect in the universe is also the start of human understanding. We could talk about God and his nature, about what happened before the beginning. We could talk of those things and speculate, and at our very best, speculation is all we have. It may be fun to speculate, but it should never be considered understanding. We can guess at the beginning, but we can never know.

What we do know is that it did get started somehow. And because it all managed to be created, we have one of two options as to how this could have happened:

1. The universe was somehow able to create itself.

2. There is an eternal, uncreated being in this universe, who being eternal, created the world as we know it.

Considering these two options, it should come as no surprise that the idea handed down to us from the earliest traditions is that of an eternal being creating the universe. It is the only thing that makes any rational sense. In fact, it makes much more sense than to believe that our universe and all it contains is the result of an accidental moment when something rose out of nothing and created itself. The more we consider the idea that the world could have been created by a series of fortunate accidents, **and** that existence rose out of nothing, **and** life came from inorganic matter, **and** the great complexity we see and experience in the world today all happened without an organizing power to oversee it, the more we must admit how very unlikely, and irrational, such a series of events would be.

It doesn't really matter which ancient tradition you consider, they all tell us the same thing: something incomprehensible created the universe. Something we do not, nor could not, understand, created all these things we know and see. That the nature and name of this incomprehensible appears differently in different stories is irrelevant to our immediate point. Our point is that something or someone beyond the grasp of human understanding created the world and all it contains.

This is the first lesson in the book of Genesis. Something beyond the reach of the human mind was there, and he made the beginning. It is a moment we will never fully understand, and we certainly will not grasp what preceded it.

God is essentially unknowable to us mortals. To him, we will always be mere mortals. This is true in not only the beginning, but also in many of the operations of the world. There is much that happens here that we will never fully understand. And that will always be.

I know of many people who refuse to believe in God for this very reason. They do not understand, they say, and so they do not believe, "How could a God?" they ask in many variations. "How could a God allow evil in the world? How could a God allow suffering? How could a God expect us to believe without proof? How could he allow the Fall? How could a good God allow sin into his creation, knowing it would produce the suffering and pain that it has?"

People ask these questions, and because they cannot conceive of an answer, they choose not to believe. They have fallen into the blunder that afflicts the intelligent; they will not believe what they cannot understand.

But this is the question I would ask in return: what kind of God would he be if you could understand everything he did? What kind of God would we have then? What kind of God would we have who submits himself to human judgment and opinion? What kind of Lord would he be if his human children were as intelligent as him, or more?

15

I think we all know. A God whom we could fully grasp and understand, whose actions we could predict and foresee, whose purpose we were able to manipulate, whose mind we could even outsmart, would be a poor God indeed. He would be no God at all.

We expect our God to be above us. He is stronger, wiser, more intelligent, and many steps ahead of anything we think or do. Anything less would not be God. So what sense does it make to deny God simply because we do not understand him? For to understand God would make him no longer God.

Perhaps that is what the unbeliever is after all along. He does not want a God that is above him. What he desires is a God below him. The unbeliever desires a God that submits to his wants and needs, his vision and desires, and most of all, to his understanding.

God never submits to our understanding. Nowhere do we see this on more profound display that in the first verse of Genesis: In the beginning.

This is the place where God confounds all human wisdom and understanding. This is where he shows himself to be God. Here is the boundary, the line of which no human mind can traverse. For before this is nothing, an empty, a void, what the Hebrews called tohu-va-vohu, the formlessness and void.

This is where our story begins. It starts with a great mystery, a great incomprehensibility. Here God began his work, of which we are not masters but a part. This is not just the beginning. This is our beginning. In the beginning, God created the heavens and the earth.

2 - Genesis 1:3-5

The Intentional Word

And God said, "Let there be light," and there was light. And God saw that the light was good. And God separated the light from the darkness. God called the light Day, and the darkness he called Night. And there was evening and there was morning, the first day.

God said, and there was.

This is the moment of creation. A divine word spoken, and the first things came into being. There was nothing, a formlessness and void. Then, a word from the mouth of God, and there is light.

This is the mastery and power of God on full display. He speaks, and his word comes into being. God shows himself the architect of the world as well as its Lord. He speaks, and it is done.

We have all seen the power of the word on display in our world. How many times is an order given and people obey? A general orders a movement of troops, and thousands of bodies converge on a given location. A boss demands an action taken, and the workers scurry to obey. A president signs a bill into law, and the whole action of a nation is changed. The word is the very method of power.

Words are powerful. A simple child's song says, "Sticks and stones may break my bones, but words will never hurt me." We know it isn't true. Words are powerful. They can hurt. Worse, and far more damaging than sticks and stones, words can wound us. Words can uplift or tear down. They can make a day our best or worst. With words a husband and wife bind themselves one to the other.

With words we bless and curse.

But who can create with the power of a word?

Only God can do this. We may dream that our word has the power of law, or wish that with a word, like magic, we can make things happen. Instead, our words require that another obey in order to carry out our wishes.

When God speaks, even the atoms obey. God speaks, and that which was not comes into being. The power of his word is total and absolute. It cannot be defied. He utters, "Let there be," and there is.

There is no fight or struggle when God creates the world. There is no Marduk slaying Tiamat in order to build the world as in Mesopotamian legends. There is no giant slowly emerging from the ice as in Norse mythology. There is no strange fornication of gods and goddesses, or light and matter to create the universe.

There is a command, and then there is. No fight. No slow building. No channeling of other powers. No need to rely upon any other spirit or being. There was a word, then there was being.

The world that God created was a world made on purpose. It was a deliberate act of a deliberate God. It was not an accident, nor was it an inevitability. It was made with purposeful deliberation.

This is more significant than most might think. It is key in our understanding of life that we realize that creation was a deliberate act. It is not always portrayed like this, and the difference can have vast consequences.

Some worldviews portray the creation of the universe as an accident. In Japanese mythology, the god and goddess, Izanagi and Izanami, have sex and the created order emerges from their union, much to their surprise. In Hindu myths, Brahman, who was thinking errant thoughts, allowed all things to come into being. And in our own secular mythology, the entire created order was a result of a great explosion and expansion that happened to emerge for no particular reason rather than it had to.

The idea that creation was an accident of some sort, or that it happened not on purpose but upon the lucky coincidence of events, makes the whole of our universe, and our existence, also an accident. Life, then, has no purpose. How can it? If life arose by the random actions of a random world, how can purpose exist?

There can be no purpose to an accident. If the world was created by accident, it is still formless and void. The very idea contradicts the possibility of purpose. We can look up at the dark and ask: What is the point of all of this? The answer is obvious: there is no point. Because there can be no purpose to a universe that was created without one.

It is not just the universe that is accidental if the universe was created by chance. We, too, would be accidents. All the circumstances that lead up to our birth, from the evolution of man up until the point of our parents meeting one another, was all the result of random chance. Events could have just as easily turned out differently. That they turned out just as they did is due to the whims of fortune.

Even if our parents decided to have a child, and our birth was the result of that happy union, it still doesn't take away the element of chance that rules over all things in an accidental universe. Our parents may have had a child on purpose, but they in no way could have planned to have us on purpose. No parent knows what kind of child he will get. No mother can have any idea about the nature of her child as it emerges from the womb. What we get, and how we are created, is also left to chance.

There can be no meaning if all is left to chance. Or rather, there can be no meaning if all is created by chance. If chance and randomness are your creator-god, then your god is blind and without meaning. Chance can have no purpose behind life except a wild experiment with the universe. If we are all here by accident, then there is no purpose to our existence.

We are caught in the opposite bind if the universe was inevitable. This is a world that, according to the laws governing its nature, made the creation of the world and all of life a foregone conclusion. Because of the nature of the laws governing the universe, it had to happen that all things came into being and developed in just the way that they did. The world couldn't help but be created, form life, and eventually make you out of the stuff of the galaxies.

This is a conclusion we have to live with if we believe that the universe is purely material. For if the world is only made of matter, and matter is ruled by the laws of nature, then matter has no choice in the way it behaves. It must act according to the dictates of its nature.

This means that the moment of creation, whatever circumstances were present then, made it inevitable that the universe would be created. The universe had to be created. There was no other way that matter could act.

And after that moment of creation, all else followed the same laws of inevitability. The planets had to form. The earth had no choice but to cool. The early chemicals that made up our world were forced to create the foundations of life. And life, once being made, was impelled forward by the iron law of survival of the fittest, thrust into a competition with all living things for supremacy of our random planet.

These same laws compel us today, They are so forceful as to make many thinkers today doubt the existence of free will. Our brains, the very vehicle of our thoughts and how we make decisions, are also governed by these irrevocable laws that rule over all the rest of nature. We cannot act except as we were made to act. We cannot think except as we were made to think. We cannot even feel except as the cold law of our nature forces us to feel.

This may be an even more dreadful universe than the random one. In this resolute world, one governed by a strict and thoughtless predestination, human beings and all our experiences are but the thoughtless impulses of a rigid nature incapable of caring about us. We are but pawns in the dealings of the cosmos, who have been given the added misery of being aware of our dreadful and lost state.

To make matters even more dreadful, our current, popular view of the universe combines both aspects of the inevitable and random universe. It is both at the same time. It is inevitable because it is run by rigid and unchangeable laws. It is random because the nature of those laws were determined by nothing other than chance. That the laws of our world act in just the way they do is the work of no one. Why do they happen to be the way they are? No reason. They just are.

All at once we are faced with the dreadful inevitability of a world that must be as it is and the vanity of a world that is just this way for no particular reason. We are forced to act according to a nature that is the way it is, just because.

The implications for the individual and his life are staggering. It should be obvious why today we have a crisis of meaning and trouble finding the joy of life and living. We are told that we are nothing but the inevitable union of atoms that were formed by rigid laws put in place by random chance. We are here because cause and effect, blindly acting, almost lashing out, had determined that you must be here. You must be here, you had to be here, but for no particular reason.

This is why the story we are told in Genesis is so important. Life, according to scripture, is not an accident.

The world is not here by chance. The events which unfolded at the beginning and led us to where we are today, were not, and are not, inevitable. All we see here was put here as a deliberate act of a deliberate God.

Life is not an accident. Neither are you an accident.

It is one of the great lies perpetuated in our culture today that life is an accident. You, by extension, become an accident as well. Being an accident, your life can have no meaning.

But this is not the truth about life. The truth is that life—all life including your own—was made on purpose. You are supposed to be here. There is meaning to your existence.

Even if your parents had no intention of bringing a child into the world or even tried to prevent a child from coming into the world does not change the fact that you are here on purpose. The God of creation only makes on purpose. He is never surprised by what forms from his work.

This idea makes all the difference in how we view life, ourselves, and others. We are supposed to be here. We are a part of an unfolding plan conceived by the mind of God. And though we may never know the extent of this plan, we can have faith that there is one. For the God that made all things—this God who is so high above us that we will never understand his intentions or purpose fully—is the God who made us as well. We were made like the earth was made. And we can look up into the stars and take comfort that we were created with a purpose in mind. And far from being a cold, random and inevitable place, this universe of ours is a place that is the work of God. Like all good works it is loved by the hand that made it, and the mind that first imagined its shape.

It was in that first moment that God said, "Let there be

light." Of all things created, light was the first of them.

This is a strange beginning if we think about it. God created light but had yet to create the sun, moon or stars. So, where did this light come from?

Many sceptics have doubted the creation story for this very reason. How stupid are these writers of the Bible, they say, when they do not know you have to have a source to have light? And so they dismiss the Bible as nothing but superstitious nonsense.

The light created in day one is not the same light that comes from the sun and the stars. Something rather different was made here. When God created the light, it was not the physical light that we see with our eyes. Rather, the light that God fashioned at the beginning was the ordering principle of the universe. It was order.

Our universe, the physical and material part of it at least, is ordered by a set of rules we have called the Laws of Nature. Without those laws that tell gravity and electricity and light how to behave, there is nothing but chaos. There is the formlessness and void, the state of things at the very beginning. What God utters forth into being at the beginning is order. He proclaims that there be a light, an ordering principle to all things. Before, there was only darkness, no guidance and direction to creation. God introduces something new. He brings light into the world. And with light comes existence.

It is this light that is the foundation and source of all things that exist. Without this light, nothing would exist. All that does exist, does so by the power of the light.

It says in Proverbs 3:19, "By wisdom God founded the world." And in John it tells us that all things were formed by the Word of God, which is the logos, or divine wisdom. The apostle also calls this Word, this reason, the light. At the very beginning, the light shines out in the darkness and the darkness could not overcome it.

The light at the very beginning is this wisdom of God. The light is wisdom, it is knowledge, it is rationality and order. The light is creative power. It is goodness and virtue. The light is joy and glory. All that is good and worthy and beautiful in this world is the light. All these things are of the light and grow out of the light. Creation itself is the outgrowth of the light. And perhaps most significantly, the light is truth.

This is not the same light that shines from the sun and stars. This is a light that needs no source, because its source is the Word of God. It shines throughout all creation. It blazes in every truth that is spoken and known. It is a light that we carry within us. It is in my heart, and it is in yours. Today, it is threatened by the dark of our unbelieving world. But it is a light that still shines and will shine until the end and beyond. Not by our eyes do we behold this light, but only by faith do we comprehend and see. And once we see by this light we are able to see things as they are.

It is this light, the light of salvation and truth, that was separated from the darkness. A great divide splits the light from darkness. Into one we have day, which is life in the light. For those who live in the day they pursue blessing and goodness. They are children of the light.

Then there is darkness and night. Without light—for that is all darkness is, the absence of light—reside all things evil. Fear, lies, depravity, perversion, sickness, despair, doubt, hate, death - these are what come out of the night. These are the virtues of the dark.

These things have been separated from the light. They will never mingle because a great divide has been set between them by the word of God. No matter how we try to make these matters relative, they will never be. Good will always be good because it is of the light. Evil will always be evil because it is of the dark. We may confuse

24

these two at times, but they are never themselves confused. Chaos and discord and fear have been separated from order and wisdom and love. They will never be the same. Our job, when seeking out the light, is not to determine what is good and right, but to uncover what is good and right. Truth is something we discover, not determine for ourselves.

We need this light to live. Just as the universe needed the light in order to be created, we need this light for life to blaze in us.

Perhaps the best way to describe or talk about this light is love. The light is the love of God. All of his aspects are tied up in this one word. For it is out of love that God created the world and each and every one of us. And his light, which shined out to form the foundation of his universe, is an expression of his love. The light that shines, that was at the very beginning, was and is the light of the love of God.

This is the dawn of creation. This is how all things came into being. And what a powerful reminder that we are given every single morning. When the night ends and the sun rises, we see the birth of a new day. We see a resurrection before our very eyes. Here is the great drama of creation played out again for us every morning. Darkness, then the coming of light. Every day, we are reminded how the light shines out in the darkness.

Without this light shining in our minds, we are bound to the shadows of ignorance and bias. We will only see what we want to see unless the light shows us truth. Our learning will always be incomplete learning, and our understanding remain incomplete understanding.

The light of truth, which shined at the dawn of our world, is the light that illumines all things, even our darkened minds. With this light, we can see with true understanding. Being committed to the light, which is committed to the truth, allows the mind to transcend even its own limitations. Ignorance is illumined, desire purged from our understanding, and if even for brief moments, we are able to see by the light that permeates all things. It is there. Truly, it shines still and waits only for minds that are committed to the truth, for those that truly want to understand.

This is the light that shined at the beginning. This is a light that shines still today. Open your eyes and see, it says. For his light shines.

3 - Genesis 1:6-8

God's World

And God said, "Let there be an expanse in the midst of the waters, and let it separate the waters from the waters." And God made the expanse and separated the waters that were under the expanse from the waters that were above the expanse. And it was so. And God called the expanse Heaven. And there was evening and there was morning, the second day.

It is the second day of creation. God creates an expanse to separate the waters. With it, he gathers waters above, and waters below, and the name of the expanse is heaven or sky.

After the first day, in which the wisdom, or the laws of creation, were laid down as the light, God starts to fashion the physical form of creation. It exists as a mass of water, and he begins by separating it into two. Water is gathered above, which eventually falls down as rain. Water is gathered below, one day becoming springs, wells, oceans, lakes, and rivers.

We see here that the form of the earth, the shape and the manner in which it will exist, is determined by God's mind and shaped by his word. This is a creation of his design. All that we see: earth, sky, sea, the principles and laws that determine their behavior—all these things were put into place by the design of God.

This may seem like an obvious and meaningless point to make. Of course, God made the world and created things by his design. But there is a deeper implication here that many of us, believers included, tend to forget.

After a while, seemingly all alone as the most gifted species on the planet, some of us fail to remember that, although the earth was given to us, it does not belong to us. We start to think that creation is here to serve us, and our authority is such that we can make creation bend to our will. We start to believe that somehow, as creatures given dominion, we are no longer subject to being a part of creation any longer. We have reckoned ourselves masters, and if the world is not to our liking, then we will make it so.

I am not talking here about landscaping, or breeding a different dog, or even draining swamps or making lakes. What I am referring to is the idea that we can change the fundamental nature of creation in order to suit our whims. I am talking about when we stretch nature too far and create something that never should be. We breed chickens so big that they die of heart attacks or cows with such huge udders they cannot walk. We suppose we can take a person born male and turn them into a woman by surgery. Or we tinker with the genetic material of a plant without considering what the long term consequences may be.

Most of us are not involved in these things. However, almost all of us, at some point or another, are guilty of getting angry at the world for not being different than it is. We may even have a righteous complaint. There are many things to be upset about today. But what we have no right to expect is that the world be any different than it is. All that exists is by the design of our God and the actions of billions of free will creatures following their own desires.

When we wish the world was different, or rather when we grow angry that the world is not different, we do not accept the simple fact that the world is not ours. This world has a master, and it is not us. We did not make the world. We did not determine its laws. We did not decide which creatures were to be allowed here. We did not fashion its shape and fill it with weather patterns and animals and tectonic activity. We did not determine who would be born and when others would die. This is not our world.

When we allow ourselves to get angry at the state of the world, there is often an assumption that the world should be a different way than it is. I bet you could even make a good argument as to why. At the same time, to allow yourself that anger admits a subtle idea that we have the authority and knowledge to say what is right and wrong with the world.

I am not talking about naming evil actions for what they are. I am talking about the greater complaint that targets the very essence of the world: why God lets certain things happen. Why he tolerates evil-doers. Why other people don't act like they are supposed to. Why life can't be like it used to. Why things have to change at all.

We even like to complain about the weather. It just needs to rain. It needs to stop raining. It's too hot. It's too cold. The sun is shining right in my face. Why are there so many damn mosquitos out here?

These are everyday complaints, and we have all made them. Most of them are harmless. But beneath them is a subtle idea that most of us ignore. When we complain, we assume we have a right to complain. When we make our gripes about the world, whether it is the weather or the government, we act as if we have the position or right to critique it. What we assume is that the world is made, more or less, to satisfy us. And if we are not satisfied with the way the world is, then this is a problem that needs to be remedied. It is a gross injustice of life that we are too hot, or upset, or have to wait in long lines. It is an offense to decency that our bills are too high and that cable TV is so expensive. It is a crime that we should grow old or were born to a poor family. It is a travesty that I can get pregnant when I have sex, even I if I don't want a child.

Not only do we complain about these things—and if it were only complaint then the sin would not be too great—we expect all these perceived wrongs to be rectified to our satisfaction. It is a high crime that we are so inconvenienced by life. And somebody needs to do something to fix it.

The implication is a hard one to bear. The world is not ours. This world was not made to satisfy us. We were not even present when the world was made.

This place, and all its attendant laws, was made by the word of God. It was fashioned for his purpose, not ours. It was laid according to his design, not ours. And it was made to satisfy his wants, not ours. Dominion may have been given to man, but the earth and the creatures within were not made to serve man. All that has been made is made to serve God. This we all have to accept.

We have become spoiled as the most gifted species on earth. Because of our dominion we have developed a sense of entitlement. In the process, our understanding has suffered. It has warped our perspective. Because we have been given authority and power over much of the planet, we have misconstrued this to mean that we have been given rights as lords and kings.

We have fallen prey to that saying, "Man is the measure of all things." It is an insidious idea that has crept into our thinking, making us believe that this universe centers around ourselves.

Man is not, as many would insist, the measure of all things. The world does not center around us, nor does it rotate around us, our wants, desires, and needs.

This is what we should learn when we read that it is God who created the heavens and the earth. The world does not serve us. The universe does not center on us.

More importantly, we do not get to determine what is

true and right, what is good and evil, what gives us purpose or not. These are not within the right and realm of man to determine.

We are creatures here on this planet like all the others. We are certainly unlike the other creatures in key and fundamental ways, but we are still creatures. This universe does not belong to us. We are not the most intelligent beings in existence. All things are not subject to the mind of man. Our thoughts and opinions do not change reality. Our needs do not make up the highest priority of the world. Things in this world do not gain their value dependent upon whether or not they are useful to us.

Man is the not the measure of all things.

That is what we are reminded of in this passage in Genesis. This world was made by the design of God, for his purpose. He alone is the measure of all things that exist and the judge of their worth. Truth is the sum of his word, not the whim of one of his creatures.

Truth is something we discover, not something we decide for ourselves. Good and evil are values that we measure our actions against, not what we choose it to be. Right and wrong have been written by the author of this world, not left to the desires of the creature. No matter how gifted we are, or how elevated and even glorified over the beasts of earth, we are not in that exalted position of creator and God.

This is our Father's world. He has given us this earth to live in and sustain us. He has even given us dominion. But he has not made all that there is for our satisfaction and pleasure. And he has certainly not made reality and truth subject to our whims.

Some may accept this truth only with great pain. Others not at all. But to all who are willing to step back and allow God the supremacy he deserves, this truth is liberating.

Take the crown off of your head. It is too weighty for a mortal head to wear. You are, at best, a creature of the earth. Blessed, gifted, and loved in a way no other creature is, this may be true. But you are still a creature. You are but one part of God's unfolding work in the world. You are precious and important to him, but do not make anymore out of yourself and your life than it is. The universe existed just fine before you were born, and it will get along just as well when you are gone. We are simply not that important. While ego may be fun to entertain, its cost is so much greater than its worth. Put it down. Be human. Whoever you are, be simply that. You will find great rest and release in the thought.

4 - Genesis 1:9-13

Life Emerges

And God said, "Let the waters under the heavens be gathered together into one place, and let the dry land appear." And it was so. God called the dry land Earth, and the waters that were gathered together he called Seas. And God saw that it was good.

And God said, "Let the earth sprout vegetation, plants yielding seed, and fruit trees bearing fruit in which is their seed, each according to its kind, on the earth." And it was so. The earth brought forth vegetation, plants yielding seed according to their own kinds, and trees bearing fruit in which is their seed, each according to its kind. And God saw that it was good. And there was evening and there was morning, the third day.

It is the third day of creation. God works with the waters again, gathering them into one place. And as the water comes together, dry land appears.

The earth is starting to receive its form as we know it. Dry land appears and with dry land God is ready to start a new phase in creation. Life is ready to emerge.

Once again, creation is spoken into being. God says, "Let there be..." and there is. This time, it is plants, vegetation, plants yielding seed, trees bearing fruit. It is no barren earth that God is working. From the first appearance of dry land, God is filling it up.

We must notice again God's mastery of the world.

Again, this is all by his design, for his purpose. Again, it is just by the utterance of a word that his will is done. It is no accident that life is present on this bountiful planet we live upon. It is by the deliberate and joyful act of a deliberate and joyful God.

God wanted life to exist. It was his will that the earth he created not be a dead creation. His work is vital, a moving, living, breathing, and eventually, willful creation.

How can we explain this thing is called life? How different life is from everything that is not alive. It can move, it can grow, it can reproduce and make others like it. It has warmth and heat, produces its own warmth and heat. Unlike a lifeless rock, it must take in nutrition. It seems to have will and desire. It hungers and thirsts. It will defend itself in fight or flight. It will even defend what it has produced.

These are all qualities of basic, primitive life. Later, we will talk about the even more outstanding human life, unlike any other living thing. But for now, God makes the most basic living things. Plants, being the simplest, come first.

It is difficult for us to properly understand what a vast and incredible miracle that is life. For something to exist at all is beyond amazing. But for something to be growing and alive astounds the intellect.

We have grown accustomed to life being here. For as long as each of us has existed there have been living things. The abundance of the miracle has numbed our sensibilities. This is just the way things are. We forget that there was a time when there was no life. We forget that there was a moment when life came into being.

Because God made life the way he did, it becomes a natural feature of the earth. He made seed bearing plants. He made trees that are fruit bearing, and in the fruit the trees have their seed. All plants are made with the elements that enable them to reproduce themselves.

This means that once made, life is able to make itself. Plants can now create more plants. Trees create more trees. The seed ensures that once the living thing dies, the species will continue.

This is not only an amazing feature of life but also indicates to us that life was created to be self-sustaining. It is natural for life to be here now. It is a natural feature of the earth to have life. And because it is a natural feature, there are accommodations made for life to continue without the constant intervention of the creator. When God made life, he didn't just make living and vital things, he made things that could have an existence somewhat apart from himself.

In some ways, we are always dependent upon God. This universe exists by his goodwill. But he has also created the life on this world to be able to sustain and perpetuate itself without his constant interventions. He has made it separate from himself.

This has become a natural feature of the earth. The independence of life is something we have grown so accustomed to that we usually fail to comprehend the full miracle at work. Human beings are very good at making things, but who can make something that can, in turn, provide for itself, sustain itself, and make copies of itself. Who can make an independent creation that can have a life of its own?

The only time we do this is when we create life ourselves. We have our own children that are made by our actions and hopefully are raised to be independent creatures. But when we do this we are only acting by the design of life that God has put in us. A child is not truly our creation, but a creation of human life. And all life must be traced back to God's designing hand.

What God has made in his mercy and wisdom is life

that can fend for and feed itself, reproduce itself, and defend itself. It can cover the planet without the intervention of the creator. One generation to the next is assured. And as conditions may alter or change, the capacity has also been given for life to adapt. To certain degrees it may alter its nature based on the circumstances it finds itself facing. While the extent of this adaptation may not be to the degree that some perceive it to be, it is nonetheless wonderful that such an adaptive capability actually exists.

In creating life, God also made it rich with diversity. It is said that the plants were made, each according to its own kind. By this we understand that when God made the plants, he didn't make them all alike. He made them unique, each according to a different kind. He made plants that grow tall and some to hug the ground. He made some that bear good food and some that are good for shade and cover. Other plants are wonderful ornaments, creating beautiful flowers and filling the air with rich fragrance. Some of the plants have medicinal uses and are good for healing. Still others are poisonous and can be used in murder.

Within this diversity he has made an interconnected balance to exist between the living things.It is a balance that gives life to the diverse species of plant and animal. The planet's health actually depends on diversity and relationship. It wasn't enough for God to make a variety of living things, he made that variety depend upon one another.

Animals are dependent upon plants for their food. But plants also depend on animals to spread seed and provide nutrients for the soil. Animals need plants to produce oxygen. Plants need animals to produce carbon dioxide. The honeybee uses nectar from the flower to make its honey. The flower uses the honeybee to spread pollen from flower to flower. These examples are only a few of the endless ways in which the variety of life on this planet is interconnected and interdependent.

It is the strange character of life that at one end it is made to be independent and at the same time it is incredibly dependent. We may not require the constant intervention of God in order to stay alive, but what we do need is the intervention of our fellow living creatures, else all life will disappear from the earth. We need plant life, insect life, animal life, the microscopic forms of life, and even human life for all of life to sustain itself on the planet. It is as if God said, "I will give you independent life. And this life is your own. But if you are to survive, then you must take care of one another."

For life to thrive, on earth and within ourselves, we must protect what God has made. True, he made our lives so that we may live independent of him. But we may not live independent of how he created life to thrive. That means, if we wish to thrive in life, we must thrive his way and not our own. He has given us free and independent lives, as he has given this to all life. But life is not such that we can do whatever we please and still expect to thrive as living things.

We are dependent on one another. Our thriving on this planet is reliant upon the survival and thriving of the other living things with whom we share the earth. To care for ourselves, we must care for them as well.

And the same is true for human life. If we wish to thrive, then we must take care of our brothers and sisters. We have been given independent life. No one will be forced to take care of anyone. You may live for yourself and your own wants and desires, and there is no force to compel you otherwise. But you cannot violate the very nature of the world. We were made to thrive in our diversity and our stewardship of one another. If you wish to do well, it is as important to look to your neighbor's good as to your own. Our life may exist independently, but our good does not. If we would do well and live a good life, it will be lived with the good of all in mind.

5 - Genesis 1:14-18

Light for the Earth

And God said, "Let there be lights in the expanse of the heavens to separate the day from the night. And let them be for signs and for seasons, and for days and years, and let them be lights in the expanse of the heavens to give light upon the earth." And it was so. And God made the two great lights—the greater light to rule the day and the lesser light to rule the night—and the stars. And God set them in the expanse of the heavens to give light on the earth, to rule over the day and over the night, and to separate the light from the darkness. And God saw that it was good. And there was evening and there was morning, the fourth day.

We come to the fourth day of creation, and God once again makes light for the earth. The sun, moon and stars are placed in the sky to shine in their respective hours. We should not be confused here and wonder at the creation of the sun on the fourth day when light was made on the first. As we have discussed previously, the light on day one was a different sort of light, being the light of wisdom and truth and guidance. Rather, the sun and stars are only sources of light by which our mortal eyes can see. The capacity for light to shine was made in day one. Now, with the sun, there is a presence of light, or source of light, for the earth.

There are three reasons the Bible gives us for the creation of the sun and the stars. These lights are here to separate the day from night, to be for signs and seasons, and to give light upon the earth.

The first two reasons God gives us for these lights is to separate day from night and for the times and seasons. This is to measure the progress of time and to be aware of the different seasons upon the earth.

It is by the movement of the stars and the sun in its rising point that we determine the time of year. The two days we call solstices, summer and winter, mark the longest and shortest days of the year. The two equinoxes, spring and autumn, indicate the two days when light and dark are equal. By them we can measure the proper time and season of the year. By these marks man can reasonably prepare for the seasons of heat and cold. More importantly, he can know when the time of planting and harvest are near. In some places, these times can mark a season of storms, or a time of nearly endless rain. To know the wet and dry periods, the planting and harvest time, the arrival of the seasons, are quite crucial to man's living on the earth as he does. These times have been set by God, and signs are given man in the progress of the heavenly lights, indicators of the coming season, so that we might know them as well.

We see here all at once an orderly God, one who made the seasons to follow a pattern that he has ordained, and a merciful God, who has given us signs that we might prosper on the earth.

God did not make the seasons random. He did not make a world in which one year we might have winter first, then autumn, then summer, and back to winter suddenly. Instead, he made the seasons of the year to progress in an orderly way. This makes it possible for man to live a more prosperous life. This enables all life to flourish. Unpredictability and chaos are conditions in which life cannot exist. This world was made orderly and, to a degree, predictable so that man and life might flourish.

Perhaps another word for the world God made is rational. He made it a world that follows laws and decrees that he has set out by his word. It is not a world that is random and spurious. It is a world of order and structure.

This is a mercy and grace of God. By this we know that God wants us to succeed at life, to flourish even. We know because he has given us an orderly universe. We know because after he ordered the universe, he gave us signs and ways that we can know and understand this sacred order.

It is not just the progress of the seasons that we measure with the lights of heaven. By these lights we also measure the advance of the years and the individual days. By these lights we measure the progress of time. And in knowing time, we know death.

Man is the only animal with an awareness of his own mortality. He is the only animal that walks around and tries to conduct his day with the knowledge residing inside of him that he will one day die. It can overwhelm us at times.

Some thinkers even speculate that all human activity is an attempt to distract us from the thought that we will die. They say that death is a horror we narrowly avoid in our minds each second that passes by and is never far from our thoughts. All of our culture and entertainment, and much of our religion, is in place to distract us or comfort us in the face of knowing we will one day die.

While I do not believe that thoughts of mortality loom so large in the course of our regular days, it is certainly something that haunts us from time to time. Most people are very good at forgetting their mortality most of the time. And if we do forget, then we have the continual reminders that will bring it to our minds again. Every year that progresses, every birthday we celebrate, the passage of time that we measure so accurately—these remind us when they come around that old age and death are progressing upon our lives.

Far from being an evil thing, this is something built into the fabric of the world. God designed the lights of heaven in order that we could measure the passage of time. He wants us to be aware of the passing days and years. God built into the world a method for us to be mindful of the incessant march of the years. God has made us, and the world, that we would know the mortality of this fleeting and mortal realm.

The Psalmist says, "Teach us to number our days, that we might gain a heart of wisdom."[1] Instead of being an awful specter of doom, the knowledge of death and mortality is a good thing. By this knowledge we begin to grow wise. It is not something we are meant to ignore but embrace.

Why would we embrace something as awful as death? Why would this good God want us to think and ponder on the destruction of our bodies?

We will leave this question for a moment, for we have not yet found death to be introduced into the world. It is still the fourth day, and man has yet to make his way onto the scene. Suffice it to say for now, the world has built into it devices for us to measure the passage of time. We, as God's creatures, are not meant to be ignorant of the march of the years, even when it forces us to think upon our own mortality.

The third purpose in creating the sun and stars is the most significant for us. God designs these sources that we might have light upon the earth.

All life needs this light. It begins with heat, warming the planet and making it possible for life to exist. Pure

---

[1]Psalm 90:12

energy rains down from the sun, touching the earth, causing weather patterns, warming the air and water. It feeds the plants, which use light to create energy. Through exposure to sunlight human beings produce the much needed nutrient we call vitamin D. Without the light of the sun, life as we know it does not exist.

Sunlight even plays a crucial role in our mental well-being. People need light to remain healthy in mind as well as body. Think about those days when the weather is overcast or cloudy, entire weeks without a sunny afternoon. Then, suddenly the clouds break and the sun comes shining through. Everybody experiences a natural lightening of the soul when this happens. We cannot help but feel a lift in our well-being when those first rays come peaking out and sun returns to our dreary world.

This doesn't even take into account the fact that by the light we see color. All the colors we see around us are reflections of the color that is already contained in the light. Every cascade of violet, every splash of crimson, every rich blue or verdant green, all of these are given to us by the light. It literally paints our world in color. Without light being just as it is, we would live in a dull and colorless world.

It would not be an understatement to say that the great light that God has given us, the sun, is the fuel and splendor of our planet. We, as created things, are completely dependent upon the light that he has made. But he has made it, and he made it for the glory of his created order. And he made it for the sustenance of his many creatures upon this earth, including us.

We cannot forget the other lights he has made as well. The lights of the night. It is often forgotten how important these are. In fact, if we hardly notice the sun most of the time, we completely forget the stars. Most of us live in places where the stars are not even visible. And if we do live in a place where they can be seen, we hardly gaze upon them. This is one of the greatest tragedies of modern life. The fact that we do not look at the stars is perhaps the main reason we do not realize the great glory of life and creation.

Almost anyone who looks up at the stars can hardly help but feel awe at the sight above them. Just as we feel comforted by the sun, we are made to feel humbled by the stars. Here we see the vastness of heaven unfolded before our very eyes. Thousands upon thousands of small lights illuminating the darkness, the deeps of space spangled and decorated with shining lights.

What great and profound thoughts are inspired by these night time lights. And what a gift we are given by them. Imagine the night without the stars. Every evening when the sun set we would have only the bleak and black cloud of night hovering over us. We would be set in a deep and impenetrable dark. We would be cast in a world of such terrible shadow that each night would be a horror.

But this is not the night God has given us. God has made instead a night that is full of smaller, though no less significant, lights. He has made the heavens at the dark of night shine with a glory visible to all. And when we are to think about its significance, we cannot help but be comforted. Because we are assured by the example of these heavenly lights that no matter how dark the night gets, there will always be the light. Even at its most terrible and darkest hour, there is still light. We are never consumed or taken over by the night. We only have to look up and be reminded that God's light is always there to shine on us. This is something that, in his wisdom, he has given us as a regular reminder of his sovereignty and love.

We can tell much about our God by considering the sheer beauty of both the stars and the moon at night. Our God has not only made the world an efficient and life-giving place, he has also made it a beautiful place. The stars and moon are two of the most significant examples. We can see that when God creates, it is more than mere function. God also creates for beauty. He has decorated his world in so many ways that should always remind us that he, too, is a lover of beautiful things. A river is made to carry water, yet it doesn't ever take the straight path, the most efficient route, one that human made pipes would. Instead, the water is carried by the meandering route of rivers and brooks that team with life and inspire us with their calm and serene beauty. Birds do not communicate through the more articulate dots and dashes of Morse Code. Instead they make song and in so doing fill a garden with music even as they speak.

Just the same, the lights that God has given us are not lights of mere function for warmth and illumination. They are lights for beauty. They are the beauty revealed by the rays of the sun which cast all things in golden light, the stars of night, arrayed like beacons in the dark sky, and the beauty of the moon who sits upon her midnight throne in serene and imperial grace, inspiring the artist and poet to capture the wonder that God has given the world.

By the lights that God has given us, we can tell much about him and much about this world he has given us. This light that illumines, that gives warmth, that brings color to the world, that gives us life—these same lights also shine to remind us that goodness and light are always shining and that this world was made to be a beautiful place.

Perhaps, we need this last message more than any other. In a world that prizes efficiency and economy over all else, we often forget important values such as beauty and wonder. Yet when God made this world, it was as much in beauty as in functionality that it was crafted. As we have grown prosperous, we have grown cheap as well.

We have valued quantity over quality and function over form. But we would do well to remember that beauty and wonder are indispensable parts of life. And we know this because they are indispensable parts of creation. God has made this world full of life and effective at producing life. But he has also made it beautiful. He has also made it full of wonder. We should remember this, and as we strive to fashion this world of ours, we should consider that the greatest thing we can do is imitate our maker, and like him, make our world a beautiful place.

6 - Genesis 1:20-25

The Miracle of Life

And God said, "Let the waters swarm with swarms of living creatures, and let birds fly above the earth across the expanse of the heavens." So God created the great sea creatures and every living creature that moves, with which the waters swarm, according to their kinds, and every winged bird according to its kind. And God saw that it was good. And God blessed them, saying, "Be fruitful and multiply and fill the waters in the seas, and let birds multiply on the earth." And there was evening and there was morning, the fifth day.

And God said, "Let the earth bring forth living creatures according to their kinds—livestock and creeping things and beasts of the earth according to their kinds." And it was so. And God made the beasts of the earth according to their kinds and the livestock according to their kinds, and everything that creeps on the ground according to its kind. And God saw that it was good.

God speaks again, and a new form of life emerges on the earth. The skies are filled with birds, the seas teem with fish, and the land swarms with insects and herds of animals. Life as we know it today is beginning.

As we read in scripture, God makes many kinds of animals. Each kind that he makes is a creature that is suited to its environment. The fish are made to survive in water, the birds in air, and the land animals made to thrive on dry land.

For one, we can see again a great love of variety in our God. He makes many types of animals and living things: fish, bird, mammal, insect, reptile, amphibian. Even greater variety is made within the type of animal too. There are species and sub-species, and within the same species there are different types and varieties.

After God creates these living things he blesses them. He gives his approval and delight to the life he made. In this blessing God gives them a command: be fruitful, multiply, and fill the earth. By this we see the will of God made explicit. God wants the earth to be full of life.

We can clearly see that God approves of life. He wants his entire earth to be filled with it. Not a corner or place or environment is to be found without some form of life. So we find life in the coldest places on earth as we find it in the deepest parts of the sea, creatures strangely adapted to the dark depths of the ocean.

The very urge to reproduce and create more life is an instinct that God has placed within all these living things. The impulse for male and female to come together and reproduce more of their kind has been observed to be almost irresistible. This is true of people as well as animals. Though some would make this impulse to be something bestial and base, a passion that degrades mankind, we do not see this in the scriptures.

The urge to sexuality is a command given by God. He doesn't merely suggest it either. He tells his creatures to do this thing: be fruitful and multiply. This is a part of God's favor and blessing, and it is also a part of his will.

The urge to reproduce, the urge of sex itself, far from being a wickedness that must be repressed, instead is a command from God. Our God rejoices in our fertility. When we reproduce we are not only obeying the command of God, we are doing his work of filling the world with life.

Sexuality is made for the fecundity of the species. We are meant to fill the earth with life. Sex and the urge to sexuality were made to guide us in obedience to the command of God. Male and female, brought together by forces they do not fully understand, as if drawn by an invisible hand, in their union produce life. It is the miracle and wonder of creation played out again in single instances by living things. It is the joy and beauty of the eternal design.

In the variety that God has given his creatures, and in every environment he has set them in, he has given them the means to survive and thrive. When it says in scripture that he made things, each according to its kind, and when we see that each creature is so well adapted to the kind of place in which it is placed, we see the favor of God on each creature. He didn't just simply set them in a place and then step back and see how well they did. No, for every creature and every place he made life, he also gave the tools suitable to thrive in each environment.

He makes the fish adapted to the sea and so gives it all it needs to thrive in water. He has made the bird with wings to thrive in the air. He has made the amphibian a sort that can thrive on land or water and so suitable to be a creature of the murks and swamps.

God has not left any of his creatures bereft of what they need. All that is required for our survival has already been given to us. None can look at the generosity of God and find it lacking. All that we need is already within our grasp. And if we were to pay closer attention, we would find that we even have what we need to thrive. God does not desire to see us fail. When he placed us here in life, he placed us here to be victors in the race set before us. Doing so, he gave us all we need to be victorious.

Finally, there is one little sentence here that has

massive importance for our life and how we view life. After all these things are created, God looks down at his creation and says that it is good. His creation to this point, all he has made with his Word, surveyed by the divine will, is declared to be good. This is one of the most important ideas we can understand in life and about life. It is good.

I think most people would agree with this if they were asked. Without even giving it any thought, almost everyone would concur with the statement that life is good. Whether or not they feel it in their hearts is another matter.

To believe that life is good, not just think, but really believe, is more important than most people realize. For what we believe about life will form the rest of our beliefs about ourselves and the rest of the world. It is something that we call a foundational belief. It forms the basis of and informs all of our other beliefs.

What we believe about life makes all the difference in what we believe about everything else this life contains. What we believe about the earth, the universe, about our fellow man and our fellow creatures, has everything to do with what we believe about life. What we believe about ourselves, our families, our work, our destiny, our purpose in life—all these hinge on the belief that we hold concerning life in general.

For if life is not good then anything that comes out life is also not good. If life is not good, then the pursuit of life is pointless. If life is not good, then much of what we call good is not good at all. All we do here is vain and empty, and there is no point, or meaning, to the struggle of all living things. The pursuit of beauty, the search for truth, the defense of all that is good and right—none of these things have any meaning at all if life itself is not good.

But if life is good, it changes everything. If life is good, there is good in us, and there is good in every other person and every other living thing. If life is good, then life is important, it has meaning, and every life has value and should not be taken spuriously. If life is good then it is a thing that should be defended, fought for, and at times, even killed for and died for. If life is good then it forms a solid basis for almost all our other values. For then we can find purpose to living.

Life is indeed good. All the life that God created was called good by divine decree. Your life is good. The life of your family and friends is good. Even the life of your enemy is good. True, he may not be living a good life. But the fact that he has life is good. Inasmuch as everyone exists as a creation of God, they are good. This should be a chief value with every single person on the planet. Life is good. Life is sacred.

Life is not a burden, as some would portray it, it is an opportunity. It is a brief and blessed opportunity that each of us is given, one which would be a sin to squander. Much of the passion and wonder that we lose in our life is due to the fact that we forget, forget in the deepest chambers of our heart, that life is good. What happens to many of us is that, because life is so abundant on our planet, we begin to think of life as something natural. And when we think of life being natural, we see it as a common thing that simply rises out of the processes of the universe.

We forget that life only seems natural to us because it was made natural on our world by God. In truth, there is nothing natural about life. The only thing natural in our universe is the formlessness and void. That God banished this dark and filled the world with light and life does not make their presence here any less miraculous. Life is a miracle. It is a wondrous miracle that each of us is privileged to be a part of.

Life is good. We must all understand this. And as we

proceed through our day, with our work and thoughts and recreation, we should proceed with this value in our hearts, that life is good.

What we believe is the fuel for our life. It gives not only direction, but motivation and endurance and the passion for daily living. And of all beliefs that we can derive strength and meaning from, few are more important than the belief that life is good.

This is what we are taught, not only from the fifth and sixth day of creation, but from every day. The lesson we are left with from Genesis chapter one, from the first book of the Bible, is the lesson that should form the foundations of our faith and belief about life. Creation is a wonder to behold, a miracle beyond miracles. And we, as living and created beings, everyone of us, are miracles as well.

Part II

-

The Creation of Man

1 - Genesis 1:26-28, 31, 2:5-9

The Creation of Man

Then God said, "Let us make man in our image, after our likeness. And let them have dominion over the fish of the sea and over the birds of the heavens and over the livestock and over all the earth and over every creeping thing that creeps on the earth."

When no bush of the field was yet in the land and no small plant of the field had yet sprung up — for the Lord God had not caused it to rain on the land, and there was no man to work the ground, and a mist was going up from the land and was watering the whole face of the ground - then the Lord God formed the man of dust from the ground and breathed into his nostrils the breath of life, and the man became a living creature. And the Lord God planted a garden in Eden, in the east, and there he put the man whom he had formed. And out of the ground the Lord God made to spring up every tree that is pleasant to the sight and good for food. The tree of life was in the midst of the garden, and the tree of the knowledge of good and evil.

So God created man in his own image,
in the image of God he created him;
male and female he created them.

And God blessed them. And God said to them, "Be fruitful and multiply and fill the earth and subdue it, and have dominion over the fish of the sea and over the birds of the heavens and over every living thing that moves on the earth." And

God saw everything that he had made, and behold, it was very good. And there was evening and there was morning, the sixth day.

Here we come to the part of our story that has the most direct bearing on our life, the creation of man. In Genesis chapter 1 we get the broad stroke of the story, what happened on the end of that sixth day. If we read further to the beginning of Genesis 2, we get the detailed snapshot. Together, they give us the whole story concerning the creation of human life.

Immediately, we can tell there is something different about this creature we call man. For one, he is the only species of animal that is named directly. All the other animals are grouped within their kind: fish, insects, birds, other animals. The Bible doesn't mention specific species in any case, until you get to man.

This tells us from the start that there is something special about this human animal. He is not created in the same stroke as the bulk of mammals that share many of our features. He gets his own mention in the creation story.

Human beings, we are told, are made in the image of God. Only man can boast of this. Other animals were made to conform to a different image, a different idea. But man, and man alone, bears upon himself the image of the Creator and God of the universe.

Much has been made and wondered about the idea that we are made in the image of God. There are no shortage of answers to try and explain what it means. I believe it would be useless to try to reduce God's image in man to one particular quality or trait. Likewise, it is pointless to try and argue whether or not this image is a physical, spiritual, or intellectual trait. Rather, I would think, since there is a great depth and complexity to God, there would be many different ways that man bears the image of his

Creator.

This is exactly what we find to be the case. Man is different from all the other creatures, and he is different in many ways. It is not in just one quality or trait that we see his uniqueness on display. Instead, it is in almost everything man does that we see he is different.

The first way we resemble God is in body. At a quick glance you can tell how different we are. Man does not walk close to the ground like the other beasts. Instead, he has an upright walk, one that is elevated from the ground. He can survey from a higher perspective than the other animals. He is immediately lifted up, and this grants a nobility to his carriage and appearance.

You may also notice how ill-equipped man seems to be. He has no fur to protect him from harsh weather conditions, nor scaly skin nor feathers. His skin is thin, and in some instances, quite pale and vulnerable even to harsh sunlight. Man has no claws or sharp teeth. He does not possess the strength that most animals have. He can neither fly nor scurry up a tree. He is one of the slowest land animals, and when he does swim, he is even slower.

At first glance he looks weaker in every aspect, the most disadvantaged of all the animals. But at the same time stands he above the animals like a king. And indeed, this is what he is. It is clear that if man is gifted, he is gifted in ways other than in his physical form.

In Genesis, chapter 2, as it describes the creation of man in greater detail, we are told that God formed the shape of man out of the dust of the ground and then breathed into him his own breath to give man life. No other creature was made in this way. All others sprang out of the ground by a command from the word of God. But man was shaped by God's hand, and the very breath of the divine was the force that animated his body.

It is the breath of God that give us, human beings made

in the divine image, our immaterial nature. Our material nature, which is our bodies, was made from dust, from the stuff of earth. But our immaterial nature, that part of us that is not made of matter, namely our spirits and our souls, are given us through the breath of God. This is how we resemble God the most, in our non-physical parts and compositions. We bear the image of God on our souls and our spirits.

Spirit and soul are words that are thrown around, often interchangeably, without us really knowing what they are. But if we are to understand how we are made in the image of God, then we need to have an idea of what these terms mean, or at least how they are understood and represented in the Bible.

The spirit can best be understood as the animating principle in a living thing. It is truly what makes something alive. Scripture tells us, "the body without the spirit is dead."[2] The spirit we possess is what gives us the vital energy of living, what makes us living beings instead of dead matter.

This is where we find the riddle and beauty of humanity. We see that we were formed out of the dust of the earth. So in this respect we resemble the animals, and in that we share many of the attributes of the beasts. Many of our instincts are like that of the animals. Our hungers, our desires, even our fears are like those of our fellow creatures. The fact that we are dependent on food and water, possess the limitations of a physical body, and are subject to the harm and deterioration of the flesh is like the animals. But at the same time, we were animated and given life by the breath of God, so we are like him too. We are both animal and divine. We are creatures of earth and also creatures of heaven.

---

[2]James 2:26

Being creatures of dust we have animal desires and passions, instincts that originate in the body and flesh. But because we are made with the breath of God we also have divine passions. These are desires and needs in us that move not the body but originate in our spirits.

Human beings are often gripped by a desire we have a hard time naming. This desire has nothing to do with our physical self. Some of the most discontent people in the world are those who enjoy the most material abundance. And hardly anyone can say he is satisfied when only his creature needs have been provided. There is a deeper desire that stirs the human animal, one that emanates from the innermost parts of our being.

What people search for is purpose. We alone want to know that this life has some greater meaning to it beyond mere survival and propagation. This desire demands that we have some significance to life, some weight or importance. It is not enough to just be alive. We want to know that our life is good and significant. What we want to know is that somehow we have contributed to a deeper meaning to existence.

This is why we are driven by moral imperatives. We want to know that what we've done is good or that we have led a good life. We want to feel like our life has made a difference in the grand scheme of the universe, that the world should be different for our being there. This is why we engage in civil and political causes. We protest and boycott and write letters to our local paper. We cry out against injustice and clean plastic waste off the beaches.

Man is an animal that requires meaning. It is not enough to simply be alive and reproduce. We crave this thing called significance. This need comes to us through our spiritual side, the divine part of us. This is the spirit moving and stirring in us, a spirit that is not content with material abundance or even the pleasures of the body.

This spirit stirs in us a passion for something greater than the life of the flesh. It draws us, continually, relentlessly, back to the God who made us.

No other animal has a spirit like this. No other creature is drawn by this particular kind of life energy—an energy that demands that it search for meaning and purpose with its life, not just survive. This is the particular energy that comes from a spirit made in the image of God, fueled with the breath of God.

The soul has a slightly different operation, though it is connected to and interchanges with the spirit. People often make the mistake of asking whether or not we have a soul. This is entirely the wrong question to ask. Soul is not something a person has or doesn't have. It is what a person is. In the words of George MacDonald, "You don't have a soul, you are a soul." That part of you that knows yourself as I is your soul. That is you. That voice that you speak to yourself with, that person deep within you, is your soul. And your soul is who you are.

The life of a man is in his spirit, but the identity of man is his soul. Together, they compose the immaterial part of us from which we derive both our identity, the power of our life, and the drives and desires that make us feel complete. It is through the soul and the spirit that we not only search for meaning but also feel curiosity and wonder. It is by the power and drive of our soul and spirit that we are lead to build civilizations, create great works of art, tell stories, explore the horizons ahead of us. It is by our souls that we ponder the great questions of life, ask ourselves what lies beyond the stars or what happened before the first moment of creation. It is through our souls and spirits that we long for beautiful things and are driven to make things beautiful. By the soul we want to know why and how and from whence did we come. We ask what the meaning of life is because our soul demands a meaning.

By our souls we feel and exercise the great virtues: courage, integrity, self-sacrifice, faith, hope, justice, and mercy. Our souls allow us to feel the pain of a fellow creature, and even give ourselves for the good of another. By the exercise of our soul we can force discipline upon our minds and bodies, even denying the self to the point of starvation. By the soul we imagine, create, attain wisdom and goodness. And finally, it is by the soul and the spirit in us we are capable of imitating God by loving one another.

This is truly how we are most like God. We, like God, are not only capable of love, we yearn for love. We feel a sense of completeness when we are not only loved by another but also when we love somebody else. Love is a great desire in man, and he does not feel like his life truly has meaning without it. This deepest impulse, not of the body, but of the spirit and the soul, is what makes us most human, and most like God.

What we call life, true life, is a life that is only found in the operations of the spirit and the soul that are generally referred to as the spiritual nature in man. Being alive, we can safely and truly say, is not the same thing as having life. What I mean is that mere biological life: breathing, heart beating, eating, cell division and the like, is not what anyone would call a real life. If we were to hear about the life of a person, and all they did with their life was eat and drink and reproduce, we would feel that they lived a miserable life indeed. Life is not being biologically alive. Life is full consciousness and purpose and desire of the soul. These are things not found in the physical nature of man, but in his spiritual nature. It is in our souls that we will truly find life and feel that our life had some significance and meaning.

The soul is that part of us that lives on after this body has grown old and perishes, following the way of all flesh. Because it is divine, like God, it returns to God. As it says in Ecclesiastes, the soul returns to God from which it came and the body returns to dust. So not only is it in our souls, in the breath of God within us, that we find the source of true life while we live in the body, it is in the soul that we hold any hope for life hereafter.

Understanding this, that both life here and life later is found in the soul, in the spiritual nature of man, it is important, indeed crucial, for man to cultivate his spiritual self. This is the seat of true life. Why, then, would we spend so much time, effort and obsession on our bodies? These bodies will not only die and decay, but they will not give us true life here and now. True life is found in the qualities of the soul and the pursuits of the spirit, not in the exercise of our physical selves.

Our work in this life should be centered around the work of the spirit. What we should be obsessed with is not how we look in the mirror, but how we exist as a spirit. Our desire should not be a beautiful body, but a beautiful soul. We should work for wisdom and virtue and goodness. We should put our efforts into those things that grant us not temporal but eternal significance. We should be exercising and cultivating that which is true and lasting life in us rather than what is passing and temporary. The work of man in this life should be a spiritual work. That is not to say that he should not do work with his hands. Some of the most meaningful spiritual work we do is with the labor of muscle and sweat. I am talking about the ultimate goals and focus of our work. Not the work we do, but what we are working toward. Our concern should be not for the health of our bodies but the health of our soul. For this is where we find ourselves. This is where we find our identity. This is where we find our meaning. This is where we find life.

Once he has been formed, a command is given to this

new, human creature. It is not a unique command at first, for it is one that was given to the other creatures as well. "Be fruitful and multiply," the Lord says. He commands us to fill the earth.

Everything that the Lord God has made is told to do this. All created beings are called and commanded to be fruitful. But none are called to be fruitful in exactly the same way. God has made each creature "according to its kind." It stands to reason that our fruitfulness is not like the fruitfulness of the other animals, but according to the kind of creature that mankind is.

On one level, we understand this command exactly as it sounds. Being fruitful also comes with the admonition to multiply and fill the earth. This is, of course, the simple fruitfulness of reproductivity. We are to fill the earth with human beings. God wants to see many of us, not just a few. Fertility is a blessing he has bestowed upon his creatures, and God is pleased to see this fertility exercised.

It was mentioned in an earlier place about the blessing of human sexuality. It should be reiterated here. Our drive for sexual relationships is a drive that is placed in us by the command of God. But it is not a drive that occurs by itself. We should not think of ourselves as creatures who mate and move on or that our job is to simply impregnate or be impregnated and to deliver a child into the world. That is only half of the command to fruitfulness.

With the impulse for fertility comes an impulse to domesticity. This is usually driven hardest by the women who bear the children, but through her the man feels drawn to this "settling down" as well. And even if he doesn't feel it as strongly at first, he usually does as the years advance upon him.

The impulse to settle down is a good one, done at the proper time. By this we don't only reproduce, we start families. And it is in a family, a unit as stable and secure as we are able to make it, that our fruitfulness is brought to a fulness that could not happen otherwise.

So, we are not given a sexual instinct to simply reproduce. We are given a drive to settle down so these children can be cared for. We are given the instincts to protect and watch over our young. We are given the impulse to shelter them and shield them, protecting them even with our own lives. Indeed, much of what we do is to secure a life for our children. Even when we go to elect leaders at the polls, we do so in mind of how our decision will effect the future of our children and grandchildren.

This is the instinct as it was supposed to work. The family is an invention of God. We can hear it in the words, male and female he created them. By this we can understand that the pairs of male and female were created by God to go with one another. And it is in this pairing that mankind derives and gains his fruitfulness. Not only in the biological sense, but also in the deeper, spiritual sense.

For when male and female come together, they not only produce the body of another human being they also provide the ideal environment for that child to be brought up. Or at least they provide the model that God intended when he created us. A family, made of a mother and father, male and female, is the relationship God intended, and was designed for both the production and the raising and guarding of the children. To have both the male and female portions of the house, to have both sexes to contribute to nurturing of the soul, is what allows for a greater completeness of the human character.

For the command we were given is not simply a command to reproduce. We are to be fruitful according to our kind. And fruitfulness for human beings looks differently than fruitfulness for any other species of animals.

For one, human beings require greater care and attention in our upbringing. We are not like the horse that can walk on its own within a few minutes of being born. Man requires attention, discipline, education, and love. And he needs both the female and male sort of love. He craves and requires both of these.

But human beings are also fruitful in different ways. We are not creatures who simply eat, sleep and mate. We are made for many other things as well. And thus to be fruitful, according to our kind, means something different and more complex than the other creatures.

Man is a creature who craves and desires to do so much. We are builders and thinkers. We are explorers and wanderers. We are artists and dancers and writers, musicians and poets. We create and imagine. We love deeply and then feel the need to express that love. We worship and glorify, we make holy and profane. We moralize, philosophize, measure, categorize, and place into schemes. We yearn to understand both our world and ourselves. Indeed, we are creatures full of wonder and energy. We are the builders of civilization and the terror of the earth.

We can be fruitful according to our kind in many different ways. When we create and build we are being fruitful according to our kind. When we teach another person or study the universe, when we write and establish laws, when we invent and tell stories, when we make movies and build roads, when we think and ponder on a subject, or allow ourselves to be moved by a painting or a poem, when we create something beautiful, or write something sublime, or utter a secret of the cosmos that was revealed to us—when we do these things we are being fruitful, and we are multiplying according to the kind of creature we are, that kind known as humanity.

There are some among us who have never fathered or

mothered children but have been, in fact, the most fruitful among us. Whether it is an artist who left a great work behind or a teacher who inspired many to learn and shaped many minds, there is a multitude of ways that people have been fruitful upon this earth. None of us were made to simply eat and mate. We were made in the image of God. And our fruitfulness is one that is made to reflect all the glory that is proper for the children of God.

To be fruitful according to our kind is to bear the light of God in our life. Not only do we reproduce, create and build, and make families, we also must stand for everything that the light stands for. This means we are to pursue goodness, truth, and justice. This means we are to seek to be wise and discerning and intelligent. We are creatures of hope and faith, shining our light amid the darkness of despair and doubt. We are to be fruitful in that we love and allow ourselves to be loved, for this is the true power of life. We are to be merciful and kind, forgiving and bearing with one another. We are to fight for the light, not only in ourselves, but in our neighbor as well. We are to cultivate the light in others, and in doing so, find true fruitfulness. We are to share the hope that is within us and in sharing uphold those who stumble. These are some of the many ways in which humankind is fruitful after the kind of creation that God has made us.

After the command to be fruitful and multiply, God gives his new humanity another directive: subdue the earth and have dominion over it. Not only over the earth itself, but man is told to have dominion over all the animals that walk the earth as well.

This is what is known as the dominion mandate. By it, many previous and present generations have justified man's mastery of the earth. This planet belongs to us, the thinking goes. It is a gift of God for man to do as he pleases. The earth and all of its inhabitants belong to man and are there to serve man. Or so goes the dominion mandate.

While there is much truth to this idea, there is much implied that is not true. The dominion mandate, unfortunately, has been used to justify man's pollution of the environment and the destruction of species. If it ever comes to a choice between preserving a species or a natural habitat, or serving the economic interests of a community, those who believe in the dominion mandate will justify the serving of economic interests based on this command. The animals and plants are here to serve man, they will say. The fields and forests and oceans are here for the benefit of humanity, the thinking will go. So, of course, we should wipe out this forest for a strip mall. Of course it's okay to endanger this species in order to put up another factory. These things we build serve the interests of man, and the earth and her creatures were made to serve man also. So the animal and plant are always pushed aside for the interests of man.

But this is a misunderstanding of the dominion mandate. Nowhere did God say take the earth and do with it as you please. Nowhere does he permit the exploitation of the earth for economic gain. Nowhere does the Bible suggest that God is indifferent to the plight of other creatures as long as the economic interests of mankind are being protected.

We treat the dominion mandate as if the earth has been given to us for our good pleasure. In fact, we are told the opposite. "The earth is the Lord's," it says in scripture, "and the fulness thereof."[3] Nor are we to believe that God is indifferent to the welfare of his other creatures. Jesus reminds us that every sparrow that falls is noted by God.

---

[3]Psalm 24:1

67

And though he also tells us that we are more valuable than many sparrows, it still stands that God has concern for even his smallest creatures.

We are not masters and owners of the earth. Mankind is but a steward of this corner of creation. The earth belongs to God, as do the creatures within it. And if it was given to man for any reason, it was given for his welfare as well as the welfare of the rest of God's creation. We are not the owners of the earth but her keepers. And if we were chosen as keepers, it was not as a sign of privilege, simply to be gifted with the earth, it was because man alone was given the gifts to make him capable of caring for the earth. We were given insight, intelligence and reason in order to figure out how best to care for this planet and its inhabitants. That is why we were given dominion, not so that we could strip the earth bare for cities and factories, cover every inch with pavement, and gorge ourselves every night until we are sick.

If we understand and acknowledge that the earth is not ours, but the Lord's, the dominion mandate presents itself in a very different way. The earth and all her creatures belong to God. Man is but the keeper. Man is the steward. This means we have been placed here on this planet, not to exploit for our own good alone but to care for all that is here with us. The command to subdue and have dominion over takes on a whole new meaning.

Subdue is the first part of the command. We often use this to mean submit. If we are to subdue creation we are to make it submit to our will. We force it to behave as we want. We will modify and breed the animals until they are completely to our satisfaction. By our power and force of will we will remake creation so that it suits and serves us.

But this is not what it means to subdue.

To subdue is not the same as to make something submit. Rather, it is a process where something is tamed and thereby made to be productive. Take a field that is overgrown with wild grass. To subdue it would be to weed and clear and plant this wild grass so that it turns into a field of wheat. To subdue is to take trees and arrange them into a grove and thereby make them more fruitful. To subdue is to take a wild animal and domesticate it. It is not to chain it to a feed lot but rather to give it broad pasture to forage, but not a limitless one.

To subdue is not to take all the wildness out of a creature, but some of it. It is to calm and tame the most destructive aspects, but leave enough of the ferocity so that the animal remains himself. It is to train the hawk to perch on our arm, but not to make it forget how to fly. It is to teach the dog to obey the whistle, but not forget how to howl at the moon. It is to domesticate the cock enough so the farmer may gather the eggs, but not so much that he no longer crows.

Subduing is a peaceful rather than violent process. It is a process whereby man gets a benefit from the animal, but the animal also prospers as well. Subduing creation makes creation more productive, not less, and in the process of subduing we do not alter the fabric of creation so far beyond its original form that it is unrecognizable. To subdue the earth makes the earth friendly and useful to man, but it is also for the good and prosperity of the earth and of all of her creatures. If our policies, as nations and people, only destroy and enrich ourselves, we have to rethink our actions. What we do as stewards of creation should be good for the whole of creation, not just those who sit at the top.

Dominion is another word that is grossly misunderstood. We, of course, hear domination. And domination is another word for us that carries with it the connotation of force and violence. While these words likely have similar roots, it is an unfortunate evolution of our language that dominion has come to mean something should not. This is a consequence of our self-centered culture.

We always tend to think of power as privilege. If someone occupies a high position, then they have the privilege of exercising their power to do as they please. Powerful men get more than the rest. They get advantage under the law and preferential treatment from our system. This has become so systemic we no longer even question it.

Corporations are given tax breaks that small businesses are not afforded. Celebrities and the wealthy are let off of heinous crimes while the average person must suffer the penalties. Politicians regularly dabble in illicit activity without consequence. Firms large enough to possess powerful government lobbies are able to get tax dollars to bail them out after unproductive years or poor decisions by management.

Our culture is rife with such instances, and we have grown so used to them we hardly protest when it happens. Power, we have come to learn, is privilege. The powerful get to do what they want. So, mankind, as the power on this planet, given dominion by God, gets to do as he wants. To the powerful goes the enjoyment of will.

But this is not what power means. This is not the purpose of dominion.

Dominion is not about privilege, nor is power. Power and dominion first exist as responsibility. It is true that man was given this dominion, and with that dominion comes power. But the reason for that power, and the reason for any privilege that we humans are granted, is because there is a heavy responsibility that comes with it. This is the secret to power and dominion that most of us have forgotten.

Every person in power is given that power in order to

execute the responsibilities they have. A policeman is given the power to arrest because he first has a responsibility to enforce the law and protect the citizens. A politician is given the power to create policies and laws because he has been given the responsibility to protect and promote justice. A CEO is given the power to terminate employees because his responsibility is to see that the company prospers. Nowhere is power given for the mere privilege of the one who holds power. In most cases, if any privilege is granted, it is done so as a necessity in carrying out those responsibilities.

Nowhere is power meant to be given for the sake of power and privilege. In fact, the opposite is true. Power is not given for the sake of the one who wields the power, it is given for the sake of those over whom he exercises that power. Even in the case of a king or emperor, he does not exercise his ultimate authority for his own sake, but for the sake of those beneath him. Power is for the protection and the security of those beneath the powerful, not for the enjoyment of the powerful.

Our culture would do well to re-instill in our leaders a sense of obligation that comes with power. Dominion and authority do not exist for the sake of those who exercise dominion but for the sake of those who are under dominion.

Reasoning this way, the dominion that man was given has a different feel. We were not made masters of the earth in order to be a privileged race. We were given dominion as a responsibility. Our responsibility is to those creatures and species that are lower than us, weaker than us, more vulnerable than we are. All the earth was commanded to be fruitful and multiply. As holders of dominion, it is our responsibility to see that other species are fruitful across the earth. That is why God gave us dominion. It is the reason he gives power. We are responsible for this earth and her creatures.

This is what it means to be stewards of the earth. That is what we are. We are not rulers. We are not kings. We are simply stewards and regents who rule in the name of the true king. We are caretakers awaiting the return of our king who is to come and claim all that is his. He has given us this responsibility—to see that the earth is fruitful—a job of ours, until he comes back.

What kind of world are we going to give back to him?

This is a question that should burn in everyone's mind, especially those in positions of power. What kind of earth are we going to give back to our God? Are we going to hand back to him an ocean full of plastic and waste, deprived of most of its life? Or will we hand him back seas and rivers full of living things, fresh and vibrant? Will we hand him back fields of concrete and strip malls? Or will we show him the abundance of forests and plains and fruitfulness of the valley? Will we give him back a sky choked with smoke and smog? Or will we greet him with clear, blue skies overhead and a clean breeze blowing off of a snowy mountain? Will we give him an earth where many species have gone extinct? Or will our planet abound in a diversity of living things, fruitful and glorious?

We are the stewards of this planet. This responsibility has been placed on our shoulders as caretakers of the earth. What kind of earth will we give back to our king when he comes back to claim what is his?

2 - Genesis 2:15

The Command to Work

The Lord God took the man and put him in the garden of Eden to work it and keep it.

We are told that God plants a garden in the east, which has come to be called Eden. This is a garden formed and designed by God, and it is filled with trees that produce food that is good to eat. Man is picked up and placed in this garden to live.

As God places the new man in the garden he gives him another command. Or rather, he gives him a job. He tells Adam that he must work the garden and keep it. And so we come to another directive that God has given us, the command to work.

Because this is a basic command, one delivered by God to the first man, it becomes a basic need and desire. When God commands us to do something, it becomes our satisfaction to please him. It becomes our joy to know that he is obeyed.

God has commanded us to work. At first it was in his garden, his creation, but we can take that to mean the whole earth he has given us. The key at first to understand is that God has made us for work. This is an essential part of who we are as humanity. We were made to work.

Idleness is one of the most destructive things for a person to experience. To sit by and do nothing, contribute nothing, is destructive for us mentally and spiritually. We were made to work, and we are happiest and feel most complete and satisfied when we have a job to do and have executed that job well. To work is a command that was given to the first man, and because it was given to him, it

73

was given to us all. Therefore, much of the meaning we find in life is in our work.

There is a misconception floating around in our culture about where and how a person finds meaning in life. Everyone wants their life to mean something and to feel like it has some significance. This is one of the primary needs we have as human beings. And at this point in history we have come to a crisis as more and more people believe that their life lacks significance.

This is due to the fact that we are searching for meaning in all the wrong places and in all the wrong ways. We have the wrong idea about where meaning and purpose come from.

What we tend to think is that meaning in life is something that is taken from life. We approach meaning like it is a resource, like gold or silver, that must be mined. We are to search it out, find meaning and purpose, take hold of it by effort of great will, and then extract it from life.

This is evident by the many pursuits we engage in to find meaning. We go out and take exotic vacations, searching for unique experiences. We take pictures by cliff sides and at exclusive resorts. We try to lean close to celebrities and superstars. We upload photos of our food and take selfies at the parties we attend. We search for that perfect job, so we can afford that perfect house in the perfect neighborhood, rub elbows with all the right people. Finally, we look to accomplish something that may distinguish us, give us the right kind of credit, and best of all, cause people to remember us after we are gone. This is what we mean when we say we are searching or desiring a life of meaning and purpose.

All of these listed above are ways that we take from life. We take experiences. We take popularity. We take fame. We take wealth. We take esteem and glory. Our search for meaning and purpose is all centered around what we can take, what we can extract, from life.

That is what is at the heart of most of our ambitions. We want to become a best-selling author. We want to be a famous actress. We want to be a renowned athlete. We want our face to be in magazines and our Twitter account to have a million followers. Today, this fame comes cheaper than ever. We need accomplish nothing for renown, simply have an Instagram account that is followed by many for no other reason than that it is followed. Just more ways we take from life.

It is this misconception that is fueling the existential crisis of our generation. We are looking for meaning and purpose in all the wrong places. Sometimes we even succeed at what we are trying to accomplish, whether in fame or wealth, but we fail to find meaning. That is because meaning in life does not come from what you take out of life, but what you give to life.

This is a simple truth: purpose is not found in what you get out of life, in experience, wealth, fame or power; purpose is found in what you give back to life. Purpose and meaning are found when we pour into life, pour into it with our very selves. We give what is ours to make life better, more complete, to add to the work of creation or aid other people in their journey of life.

The best way we do this, to give of ourselves, is through work. That is what work is—a contribution of ourselves to life. When we work we are giving our time. When we work we are giving our ability, our concentration, our effort to whatever our work is.

It doesn't matter that most of us get paid for our work. It is poor exchange when all we get for the gift of ourselves is a few dollars, some slips of green paper that are only good for trading for other things. It is small compensation to get only money for work. And it doesn't change the fact that work is a gift of the hours of our life.

Work is one of the most fulfilling things a person can do. Not only in work do we get to claim our fair share of the bounty, but in work we know that we contribute to the well being of society. It isn't just financially healthy to work, but psychologically. Everyone feels better about himself when he is working. Sometimes, even if we are feeling bad, we can go out and engage in labor for a few hours, gardening or cleaning, and feel better when we are done. The satisfaction from a job well done is a satisfaction that is unlike any other.

Work is also the way in which we change the world. This is something everyone wants to do today. Go out, we tell kids when they graduate, and change the world. But we fail to tell them the most effective way to do that. To change the world, we must work. Indeed, there is no change to the world without work. More effective than any marches, slogans or protests, your work, though it seems trivial, like simple cleaning, has changed the world. When you sweep a floor you have made the floor different. When you make a cabinet you are arranging the wood in a new way. When you teach, you are altering minds. When you apply medicine you are changing sickness into health. When we work, true work, we change the world.

It should come as no surprise that work is so important to us and has such a powerful impact on the individual life. It should come as no surprise because work is a command given to us by God. It is an impulse that touches us in the deepest part of our being. A stirring resides in the heart of every man, woman and child that compels and draws us to action. We long for work because we were made to work. In the ancient core of our being still echoes the command given by no other except our God and our Creator. Though we may resist, we do so at our own peril. It is such an essential part of our being that we do not exaggerate when we say man's happiness is incomplete without work.

The work that man is given to do is not just any work. When God put Adam in the Garden and told him to work he didn't ask him to find something to do and do it well. There was a specific task that Adam was given, a specific work: keep the Garden.

Adam was told by God to work the Garden and keep it. We don't know if any other instructions were given. We don't know if any details were added to this. All we are told is that Adam was ordered to keep the Garden. Work it and keep it were his instructions.

What we can determine from this is that the first man was not only given work to do in life, but a specific form of work. His work is to keep and continue God's work. Our Lord was the one who planted the Garden, and he asked man to continue that work.

The Garden is no longer ours to inhabit, but the rest of the earth is. We have the world, we have our fellow human beings, and we have ourselves and all that God has given us. All of this is also a work of God. All of this is part of his Garden. Everyone of us is included in the plan of creation as it stands, just as that special Garden was. Our work is to keep and work what he has given us.

Each of us, as a creation of God, can consider himself a garden. Or rather, we should consider and understand that God has given each of us a garden as he gave Adam a garden. It doesn't look like Adam's garden, nor do ours look like anyone else's. We each have our own garden, because we are each separate and distinct creations of God. My garden is not the same as yours, nor yours like another person's. You have distinct character traits, talents, tendencies, thoughts and emotions. You have a combination of gifts and traits that come together in a unique way. This is your garden.

We have all been given something like this, and God has commanded us to work it and keep it. When it came to us, as children, it came in a raw form, uncultivated and untamed. But it is ours, to have dominion over, to cultivate and to use.

To work something is to apply discipline and labor so that, not only will the form of what you're working be changed, but the potential will be increased. Think of it like an unplowed field. To work that field is to plow, plant, then to care for and weed. Then you harvest the field, and with that increase plant it again for it to keep producing.

To leave something unworked is to let it stagnate, and in stagnation it never reaches its potential but instead begins a slow and inevitable decay. A fruit tree that is never pruned will only offer a small yield. A hunting dog that is never trained will not realize the usefulness for which it was bred. A human being that goes untaught and undisciplined will never rightly grow up. Uncultivated, he will never reach his potential or even come close to it. He will be an organism that exists only to exist. He will be helpless and greedy, grasping but incapable of taking hold of anything for himself. In a word, an uncultivated person is summed up in that one word—spoiled.

What a perfect word that is for an undisciplined, uneducated, uncultivated person. Spoiled. One thinks of milk that is left out too long. It has soured and become unpotable. It is good for no one.

The same is true of people. A child who is never given discipline, who is never educated, who has never had to labor or earn for himself, is just like that milk that has sat too long. He is spoiled, good for no one and for nothing. He is not even good for himself.

For anything to be useful it must be cultivated. This is true of plants as well as animals. It is also true for people.

The earth and all it contains must be worked, it must be kept, in order to be useful and effective. Nothing can reach or achieve its destiny without work and cultivation.

As we engage in this work, as we cultivate our gardens, we must also remember the other part of that command, the part that tells us to keep the garden as well as work it. Everything must be worked and cultivated to reach greater use and potential. Everything also must be kept—maintaining enough of its native form and function that it isn't stretched beyond its nature and destroyed.

The gardens we are given—all of our gifts, talents and traits—are given for us to work them. We work them to train and discipline ourselves. We work them to be refined and sharpened. We work to maximize our potential. But we also work to do these things in an upright and righteous manner. In this way we work the soul and the spirit, to increase its goodness and efficacy, and take the kernel, the seed of humanity that God has given each of us, and husband this to its greatest possible yield. To do this is to cultivate the unique image of God that resides in each of us.

But we also remember to keep what God has given us. To over-cultivate, over-train, and even over-discipline, can often destroy the native strength and ability we were given. To over-work a garden is to give up some of its wildness, and in so doing lose some of its vitality as well.

We should always leave room for a bit of the wild. A garden that is too controlled looks artificial. A soul that is too tamed suffers in its vigor. For a tree to grow too wild makes it less productive. But for a tree to be pruned too much robs it of strength and potency.

In the same way, as you work the garden of the self, apply discipline, teaching, and instruction. Strive to tame the strange abilities and emotions within you, and by taming, cultivate them to greater use. But as you do that, be sure to keep the native form that God has breathed in you. Leave some room for wildness to grow, a part that will always remain untamed. And in each of us will grow that sacred garden, given to us by God to keep and work, always producing abundance, but always maintaining a primitive power and potency that is our natural condition.

3 - Genesis 2:16-17

The Forbidding

And the Lord God commanded the man, saying, "You may surely eat of every tree of the garden, but of the tree of the knowledge of good and evil you shall not eat, for in the day that you eat of it you shall surely die."

In this passage God gives man the first true law. He gives it as he also permits. Of any tree you desire, the Lord tells Adam, you may eat, except for the tree in the midst of the garden. If you eat of that tree you will die.

Consider the great freedom man is given here. Nothing is forbidden except for one thing. Of course, today, there are many things forbidden. But this is a result of man's multiplying of sin rather than God's withholding nature.

We tend, though, to notice only those things that are forbidden to us. Our desire is always naturally drawn to what we can't do. We will complain about what we are not allowed and fail to see the great diversity of things that are allowed. Adam was given all of the trees to eat from. He was only forbidden one. We are given this great wide world and all its variety to find our nourishment and happiness. Why is it we will grieve those few things we are not allowed to have?

Man in general is a free creature. In will he is free to do anything within his capability. By the decree of God he is permitted to do anything not expressly forbidden by command. We are free to do as we will, to do as we see is right, except those things that God has forbidden. And as much as we like to moan and complain about the unfairness of being forbidden that which we want to do, we shall see that forbidden fruit is not banned to deny us pleasure, but to save us from death.

This command that God gives Adam teaches us about the nature of sin. In previous places God had given other commands. He told man to be fruitful, he told him to subdue the earth, and he told him to keep and work the garden. But this command is different. To recognize the difference between the two, and why they are different, is to understand the nature of good and evil.

To carry out those commands, the ones God first gave us, is to do good. For God is the source of good and life. If we were to not do what God commands us: not multiply, not subdue the earth, not keep the garden, we would not necessarily be committing evil. Perhaps we may call this a sin of omission, but we would not call it evil. We would be guilty of not doing good.

We all usually recognize that there is a difference between good and evil. What we don't always regard is that middle place where we do neither good nor evil. It is this very place of mediocrity that many of us occupy. We are not out in the world doing those things that God has forbidden, so we congratulate ourselves on being good.

But refraining from evil is not the same as good. Nor is refraining from good, evil. A man can sit on his couch and watch TV all day, completely minding his own business. He has done no evil from that perch. But neither has he done any good. To do nothing is to stagnate. And while it may not be evil, and some console themselves with this minor achievement, it also is not good.

To do good one must be engaged in the action of obedience. Good is not passive. Good requires that we move and act, go out and work—subdue, and fill the earth. To do good requires our deliberate and active obedience.

Anytime we obey God, do what he has told us to do, we do good. When we do good we are doing the work of life.

When we do good we increase the life in the world and we increase the life in us. Because doing good and obeying God actively are the same, it is also continuing the work of God. That is what makes an action good. Good works, all types of good works, continue the work of God. And the work of God—at least as far as we can see—is the work of building life.

So, when we do active good in the world, we are not pleasing the arbitrary commands of an arbitrary God. We are finishing, or participating in, his work. His work is life. And when we do good, we build, encourage, and sometimes even help begin life. This is what makes good, good. God's work is that first good, clarified by his decree, "it is good." And so to continue that work is also good. When we do good, we give life. When we do good, the great quest and journey of life is continued on earth.

This new command that God gives Adam—do not eat of the tree in the midst of the garden—is different in two ways. The first way is that it is a negative command. Unlike the others, it does not tell us what we should do, but what we should not do. The other difference, the most distinct, is that this command comes with a consequence. If you eat of this tree, the Lord tells Adam, in that day you will die.

In the previous commands, were we to disobey, then we would fail to do good, and thus fail to work life in ourselves and the world. In this command, if we do what God has told not to do, then death is the result.

This is sin: disobeying God's will in those things he has forbidden. Sin is disobedience that leads to death.

When we fail to do good, fail in those commands God has given us for what is good, we fail to work for life. Life does not increase in us nor does it increase in others. When we fail to do good, the result is stagnation. Our growth and wisdom is stunted. And because we do not grow we experience a slow rotting of the self. But we are not committing evil. We may be guilty of ignoring God's command, and so reap the results of stagnation, but we are not committing sin, or bringing about death.

But when we disobey and do what is forbidden by God, we do those things that result in death. We actively work death in ourselves and the world around us. Sin is anti-life. Sin destroys life. Sin is the worker of death in the world. As we shall see later, sin is the cause of bringing the first death into the world. It is by our continual sinning that death is perpetuated and maintained.

When we complain about those things that God has forbidden, we are complaining that God will not allow us to pursue death. We look at God's commands as the decrees of an angry and stuffy God that does not like to see young people enjoy themselves. We see God as a curmudgeonly old man, chasing kids off his lawn because their laughter has disturbed him.

The truth could not be further from this. God does not forbid us from sin to be arbitrary or withholding. He forbids sin because he desires life in us. God wants us to live, and to live abundantly. He forbids sin because sin is death, and when we sin, when we disobey and do what he has forbidden, we work death in ourselves and in the world around us. Sin is a toxin to the soul. Sin is a poison of the spirit. It is an elixir of death that we, in our blindness, mistake for the wines of happiness. When we sin, we open the gates of death into our life and we work un-life in the world.

This is what makes sin so terrible. It is common today to judge an action by its results on other people. We will ask, does it hurt anyone? And if the answer is no, then we declare that action good. Does it cause pain to another person? If not, then permit me to do it.

What we fail to realize is that sin, all sin, does cause

pain. It is hard for us to see because we live in a world of death. All of us, bound by sin to this mortality which robs life of us all, have a hard time recognizing the death that sin reaps, because death is the strong reality of our existence.

If we were to possess more innocent eyes, then we would see the truth. We would see that sin, all sin, no matter how seemingly harmless, works death in the world. First, and foremost, it works death in the sinner. It may not look like anyone is harmed by these "victimless" crimes, but we fail to see that the victim is the perpetrator of those crimes. To sin, and continue to sin, is to die slowly, moment by moment, act by act. To sin is to try and nourish ourselves on the toxin of our own perpetuated evil. As we consume, the image of God within us becomes distorted, perverted, and destroyed. It is by sin that we destroy ourselves.

If this was all, that should be warning enough to avoid. But sin, even personal and private sin, does hurt others. We, as human beings, are not creatures that belong to ourselves. We belong to God. We are his creatures and a part of his world. In this place, all life is interconnected. We have been given influence over creation by God's command. His order to subdue, multiply and keep his work gives us not only authority over his work but also a deep and abiding connection to it. In other words, what happens to us has an impact on the world and the people around us.

So, when we sin, we are not only inviting death into ourselves, we are bringing death to creation. We harm all creation, because we are connected to creation. When we bring death to ourselves, by that connection, it emanates from us and infects the people around us. It even touches the earth itself. Sin is not just death for us, but also death to others. Sin is never a victimless crime. By sin we work against God and sow death in a place that he has meant for life.

We will see this play out in the following chapters. As soon as sin comes into the world, it is not just a contagion that causes the corruption of humanity. It is a disease that will infect the earth, the creatures of the earth, and even the beings of heaven.

4 - Genesis 2:18-20

The Search for a Helper

Then the Lord God said, "It is not good that the man should be alone; I will make him a helper fit for him." Now out of the ground the Lord God had formed every beast of the field and every bird of the heavens and brought them to the man to see what he would call them. And whatever the man called every living creature, that was its name. The man gave names to all livestock and to the birds of the heavens and to every beast of the field. But for Adam there was not found a helper fit for him.

Creation is nearly complete. All the animals have been made. Man is created. A garden is planted for man to live in and he is given his job and role on earth. We are made to believe it may all be finished.

But then God looks down on his creation and sees something not right. All has been declared good, and it is good. Only one thing is out of place. We hear for the first time that something isn't good. It is not good, God says, that man is alone.

Man is not meant to be alone. Some might hear this phrase and see that human beings are meant to be social animals. And this is certainly true. Except in this place it seems that the Lord means something else.

When God sees that man is lacking something, he observes that what he needs is a helper, a partner. Man needs someone with whom he can share his burdens and his life. He needs someone who will walk with him through all the valleys and mountains of life. He needs someone at his side.

To solve this problem the Lord brings all the animals that have already been created to the man. The search is to see if there is among those creatures a helper and partner that is fit for the man. As the creatures are being presented to Adam, God asks the man what he would call the animals. And whatever Adam calls them, this becomes the name of the creature.

A great honor is bestowed upon the new man. God has allowed him to name the creatures. Whatever the man calls them, that is its name. God could have easily insisted on naming the creatures himself, and that would have been within in his prerogative. Instead, he allows man to do it.

In allowing man this right, he is affirming the authority that Adam was given over the earth. The earth and all it contains belong surely to our God, but the authority and dominion to oversee creation was given to humanity. He was made preeminent over all the creatures, and nowhere do we see this on display as much as when God allows Adam to name all the creatures that God made. It is God's way of affirming that the direction of the earth will be in man's hands, and he is to take hold of it with little interference from God.

Despite having ultimate power, he chooses to give authority to man. He is a hands-off manager. Once the promise of dominion is given, it will not be taken away until it is necessary. How man executes his duty will be left up to man. The earth is his show to run, God will not be the type to demand constant intervention. Instead, he will allow the fledgling master of the world to operate under his own power and will. This is God's style of management on display.

In giving man this opportunity he is also allowing him an incredible amount of freedom and trust. This is God's creation, and he is placing it in human hands. Adam, and all of his offspring, have the freedom to make their own mark upon the world, to exercise their power as they will. There is no coming down to intervene when he is about to make a mistake. And if there is a wrong to be corrected, then it is up to him to correct that wrong.

God is known as an omnipotent God. This means he is all powerful. He can do anything he wants to. There is nothing, as far as we know, that is beyond his ability. But he is also a God, though omnipotent, that restrains his power. In fact, God's relationship to humanity, in many ways, can be characterized by God constantly restraining his power towards man and the world.

The first real instance where we see that restraint is when he gives Adam the privilege of naming the animals. These are yours to name, God says, I will restrain my privilege and authority. I will pull back my power in order that you can exercise your dominion over the earth and over yourself. I will allow you to be.

This is a privilege that God continues to extend to us. God continually restrains his own power and he does it for our sake. Without that restraint we would not be able to exercise or experience free will.

In exercising total and absolute power, all things would be under the direct will of God. All that happened would be forced by the movement of his hands. All of our actions would be compelled by his will. Our thoughts would even succumb, and not be our thoughts, but the ideas put into our minds by the irresistible hand of God. Even our feelings would be subject. If God exercised his omnipotence, our emotions would be but the feelings that God willed us to feel. There could not be a single molecule in all of creation that could resist the impulse of God's irresistible directive. Every moment of creation would bend to his command.

What then would become of man? He would be a puppet, an automaton, a mere robot or program following the commands given to him. And though some may argue that we are just such creatures, this is not the kind of creature that we see God making in Genesis, nor is it the kind of God who is making all things.

By giving man dominion, and allowing him to name the animals, which is an exercise of that dominion, we see a God that restrains his power. He is all-powerful, but he does not exercise this power. He pulls back on it, reigns it in. And he does it so man can exercise his own power. He does it so man can have the dominion that God has given him. Whatever the destiny of humanity might be, this freedom to exercise our power is critical.

It is an incredible act of love to allow mankind to be an independent and independently acting creature. God has made us like himself, and he desires us to do good and seek after him. But he has forced us to do none of these things. Instead, he gives us freedom, he gives us choice, he gives us his will and his teaching; then he steps back and allows us to do with it as we will.

It is an incredible act if you think about it. God could have made this world to be perfect and perfectly abiding by his will. He could have made it without a flaw. Instead, he made us free. He gave us power, shared some of his own, restrained himself, and allows us to discover and shape ourselves.

Many people have noticed that God is usually a hidden God. By this, I mean his presence and existence are not immediately obvious. We have to wonder and debate about whether he exists. And for those of us who do believe in God, we are required to have faith.

We often long for a God who reveals himself in dramatic and obvious ways. We would like him to talk to us in appearances of radiant light. We want guarantees and assurances that he is here watching over us. We want God to be obvious and apparent.

Instead, we get a hidden God. We get a God who makes us seek and search after him. We get a God that requires faith, and not sight.

Almost every believer complains about this at one time or another during his life. We don't always appreciate the hidden God. What we fail to understand is that God's hiddenness is for our benefit, not his. If God was not hidden and withdrawn, then we would be unable to live as independent creatures with independent wills. If God were to show himself and reveal his presence, we would be so overwhelmed by the sheer scope of his power that our wills would be consumed by his. The magnitude and power of his being would overwhelm ours, and our own self would be washed away. Our personality would cease to exist.

We could never really grow as independent creatures without the freedom and independence that growth requires. Could we learn right from wrong if God's hand continually restrained us? Or how could we truly learn what was good if our minds were not our own?

God's restraint and hiddenness is for our benefit. Drawing himself away, he is giving us room to be and to grow. He is allowing our character and personality to form. He is letting us learn good from evil, not because we are told that it is good, or that we are punished for evil; he is letting us learn good from evil in its own right, that we can discover and know it for what it is, and take ownership for what is good and right. Instead of merely telling us what is right and good, he is letting us discover ourselves. For in that self-discovery, we understand better the depths and rightness of what he has called good.

Yet, by allowing us this freedom, God also allows us to

make mistakes. We take full advantage of this freedom. Some of the mistakes have been horrific. Some of them have been nightmares. And still, God allows them.

By this we can conclude that either God is not there, or that he knows that the mistakes are worth the risk. We may shudder at these mistakes, but we have to realize that they are our mistakes, and not God 's. We have despoiled the earth and murdered one another. We have perpetuated evil, and even cheered it on. We have executed and allowed genocide and pogroms and tyranny to fester on the earth. These are the crimes of man, not of God.

God has given us this freedom; the freedom to make mistakes. However, we should not focus on the ability to make mistakes, rather the freedom he has given us to shape who we will be. He has allowed our personalities and selves to flourish and grow, and he has allowed us this room. In this freedom, we find one day, that though we are independent creatures, we need him very much. We find that though God is hidden, he wants very much to be revealed, and awaits the day, when realizing that need, we invite him into our lives. And as we grow into that freedom, and become more the men and women we were made to be, also discover that the hand of God had been upon us every second of our lives, guiding and directing us as we are willing, hidden, but never for a moment absent.

This is an incredible gift—dominion over the earth, freedom as independent creatures—to do as we will, for good or evil. It is also a frightening gift. All we have to do is look at the consequences of our dominion and freedom, and we can see that it doesn't always turn out well. It is a gift, and it is also a burden.

This is not a burden any of us were destined to bear on our own. God sees the great weight this dominion and freedom cast upon the man. Perhaps, this is what caused him to look down upon Adam and say, "It is not good for man to be alone." This is why man needs a helper and a partner.

No one person is made to bear the burden of life alone. It is, as God truly says, not good to be alone. Our dominion, our freedom, cries out for a partner, a helper, to walk with us and navigate the difficult task of freedom and the weighty burden of dominion.

Of all the animals God brings to Adam, none of them are found as a fitting partner and helper. Someone else will be needed to help Adam and share with him the weight of dominion and freedom. To be a fitting helper and partner for Adam's unique burden will require a unique act of creation.

5 - Genesis 2:20-24

The Woman/First Marriage

So the Lord God caused a deep sleep to fall upon the man, and while he slept took one of his ribs and closed up its place with flesh. And the rib that the Lord God had taken from the man he made into a woman and brought her to the man. Then the man said,

"This at last is bone of my bones
and flesh of my flesh;
she shall be called Woman,
because she was taken out of Man."

Therefore a man shall leave his father and his mother and hold fast to his wife, and they shall become one flesh.

After seeing all the other animals, a helper is still not found for Adam. He names all the animals, he sees them all, but something was not right about each of them. None of them were suitable as a helper. As useful as the animals can be for us, as much as they can help us, they are not, none of them, our true helpers. They can help us with labor, but they cannot help us with life.

So the Lord sets out to solve this problem and create a helper and partner, one just right for Adam. He causes a deep sleep to come upon the man, and while asleep, removes a rib. Out of this rib he forms the woman. We come to know this woman as Eve, the mother of all.

The world and all the creatures in it were made by the word of God, with a single utterance. But the man and woman are made in unique ways. Adam was fashioned from the earth and the breath of God, and Eve was formed from the rib of man.

Neither the human male nor the human female are like any of the other creatures in the world. Both sexes of humanity stand apart in their dignity and souls from the rest of creation.

The woman, we find, is a special and extraordinary creation, just like Adam. There is no other creature like her in all the earth. This is the partner and helper that God made for Adam, and as it turns out, she was perfect for him. The first time Adam sees her, he falls immediately in love. His eyes behold the face and figure made specifically for him, and he cannot help but feel an immediate and overwhelming desire.

It should come as no surprise then, that the desire men feel for women can be so intense. She was made for man, designed specifically for him. God would not have created a form that was repulsive to the man. Instead, he made her with the fate of future generations at stake. And there is hardly a man alive who does not marvel, does not feel in awe, when they are faced and confronted with feminine beauty. It is right that he should feel this awe, because this woman was made to impress him. This is the design of our Lord for the lonely man. There is an awakening of the soul when man sees woman for the first time and falls under the enchantment of her beauty. Even as abused and corrupted as that desire is today through the scourge of sin, it is, at heart, a good desire. Some would even call it an irresistible desire. At the least, it is difficult to resist, for this is the design of our God, and the woman was designed to be desired by the man.

Adam falls immediately in love. As he awakens and sees the woman for the first time, he reacts as young lovers often do—he composes poetry. "Here at last," he says, "is bone of my bone and flesh of my flesh." That is his way of saying, you were made for me. You are perfect for me. In fact, you are so perfect, you are a part of me, a missing part of me. With you, I am now complete.

Many young men have made a similar claim. They declare to the woman they love that the two of them were made to go together, that it feels as if she is a missing part of himself. In the case of Adam, this was literally true. So when men feel that intense longing for a woman, that desire that can best be described as incompleteness, they only act as their forefather, who searched and longed for that one to make him complete. Bone of my bone and flesh of my flesh.

Together, Adam and Eve make the first male-female pair, designed by God. This is the first marriage, and from it is formed the model and form that all marriages are intended to follow. We are shown what a marital union is supposed to look like. How the individual couples decide to live out their marriage is up to them, and there are many types and forms that can be happy marriages. There is variety and choice within married relationships. However, to be a marriage that fulfills the purpose of marriage that God created it to be, it has to reflect and follow the design that was fashioned at the beginning.

The first intent of marriage is that it be a helping relationship. That was the inspiration for the idea in the first place. This is where so many people in the West get marriage wrong from the beginning. We have been so overtaken by the aspects of erotic love present in the marriage that we have allowed it to overshadow everything else. We have made the marriage all about those intense feelings of being in love. And while those feelings are certainly desirable, they are in no way supposed to be the foundation of a marriage.

A marriage was designed to be a partnership, a

relationship of help. That intense feeling of love is often the motivation, and it is also often the reward of the relationship, but it is not the purpose of the marriage. The union of man and woman was made to be a relationship whereby they provide help and support to one another.

Woman was designed and made to be the partner of man as he struggles and navigates through life—through all of life. Through ups and downs, victories and defeats, good times and bad times, they were meant to stay together and help each other through life. That is why the traditional marriage vow sounds like it does. You vow to stay together through those tough times because it is in those very difficult times that you need a partner the most.

Life is difficult. God saw that this was to be the case early on. It is a struggle that touches us and confronts us no matter who we are or what privilege we were born to. To ease the pain of this struggle, God has made a partner for us. Just as we were made to confront the struggle of life, we were also made to go through that struggle with a partner. We were not made to face life alone. God has made for us a helper to ease the burden of life. And together, man and woman are joined to face not only all the difficulties of life but also experience all of its joys.

In this first marriage, in the joining of man and woman, we see God at work here as he combines a beautiful mix of opposites. He creates a male and female, two types of the same species. On the surface, we can see the physical differences between the two, and as we observe further, we begin to see a spiritual difference as well.

But the opposites that God creates in the male-female pair is not like the kind of opposites that destroy or contradict or cancel each other, like fire and water. The kind of opposite you see in the male-female bond is the kind that complements one another. They do not cancel one another out, rather they are catalysts for one another. Coming together, they create life. Out of this bond, this combination of two different types, new life emerges.

Scripture uses the term, one flesh, to describe what happens. The two become one flesh. On the surface this is a description of sexual activity. Two bodies are temporarily joined, and the union produces human offspring. But there is also a deeper, spiritual intimacy that cannot be ignored in this union.

What happens in the body is a symbol of what happens with the spirit. That is why the apostle Paul warns the Corinthians about sexual congress with prostitutes. He wasn't concerned about a brief, physical joining of bodies. What was dangerous was the real spiritual bond formed in sexual activity, the two flesh becoming one. It is a real bonding and joining, one that occurs despite the amount of promiscuity involved. And such promiscuity is discouraged by scripture in part because of the real spiritual bond that occurs during sex. The complex web of spiritual bonds we create, or the bonds we create with unhealthy or destructive people, is the awful consequence of a promiscuous society. The effect is more destructive on the woman, who feels the bond more intensely, and seeks strength from that bond, when joining herself to those who are not committed to her good, but only their own pleasure.

Followed through and practiced properly, this bond is a gift and a blessing. Though it is a bond that can exist in any male-female pairing (and only male-female pairings), it is one that only thrives when the man and woman are suitably committed to one another. None of these bonds will be perfect, but all will be life-giving if pursued with loving intent.

We can see what great things come out of this pair bond of male and female. Not only is physical life created—which in itself is a miracle—but spiritual life is also created and increased in this beautiful, sometimes tempestuous and tormentful, bonding of opposites. Two parts, two sides, the male and the female coming together, and together they create life. No one would want to be without the other, and thus incomplete. It is indeed a mystery, and indeed a gift.

6 - Genesis 2:25

Life without Shame

And the man and his wife were both naked and were not ashamed.

Creation, at last, is nearing completion. In many ways, we can say that creation is still happening, still ongoing through the development and changing state of the earth and humanity. But as far as God's direct and original work of creation, the story is almost complete. The heavens and earth have been given shape, the land and sea filled with life, and the overseer of all this work, Adam, has been appointed, and a helper, Eve given to him. The earth and humanity rise up in their infant days to live out the plan and purpose of God. In the final verse of Chapter two, we are given a one sentence description of the state in which Adam and Eve lived. They were naked and they were not ashamed.

Naked and not ashamed. It is a brief description, but tells us that our forebears existed in a state of original bliss. It is a child-like state, one of innocence that knows neither sin nor shame.

They had yet to sin, and so could feel no guilt. This is because they had yet been given a law concerning right and wrong. As such, they had no knowledge, no concept of what we call right and wrong, good and evil. So they were innocent. It was an innocence like a child's. Children often do what we call wrong, yet we do not hold them accountable as we do adults, nor do we reckon them guilty. For example, kids are known as natural thieves, for they will take anything they desire. Yet we do not consider them thieves, or evil, because of it. It is because they are innocent of such matters. Because they do not yet understand between right and wrong, we do not consider them capable of bearing guilt.

Most of our courts work with the same understanding. If a person who is convicted of a crime is shown to not be able to understand the difference between right and wrong, we consider them cleared of guilt. If it is determined by the court that the accused did not have the capacity to judge the rightness of his actions—because of a disability in learning, or youth, or a state of insanity—then that person is cleared of the charges. It is not because that person did not do the things he is accused of, but rather he is innocent on account of not knowing that his actions were evil.

This is the state of innocence that we occupy as children, and this is the state of innocence in which mankind originally existed. Adam and Eve were innocent because they did not know right and wrong. There was only one wrong for them, and they had yet to commit it.

So, in our original, created state we did not have guilt. Without guilt, we had no shame. Adam and Eve were naked, we are told, and they felt no shame at that nakedness.

This is significant, for there is no state that we can be in that induces more shame than to be naked in front of others. We feel vulnerable, exposed, at the mercy and judgment of others. It is no accident that during execution, many cultures strip the condemned, thereby exposing them to the public eye, and their guilt is laid bare.

But in order to feel shame, we must have a sense of both vulnerability and inadequacy. Shame is a combination of both of these. First, there is a sense that we are inadequate, insufficient. There is a flaw or weakness in us that we do not wish others to see or know about. And why do we want to keep our inadequacies hidden from others? It is so we can maintain a sense of pride and worth. If others do not see my weakness and inadequacies, then I can keep up the illusion of my worth. And we all want to feel worthy. We want to feel that confidence and certainty that we belong, we are important, that our life is meaningful and has purpose. To feel pride in our life is to feel these things.

But to feel shame is to have all of these good and confident feelings stripped away from us. It is not only present when we have done something wrong, it can be present when we are just made to feel small or inadequate. Our weakness is exposed, our inadequacy laid bare. All the ways that we are less than good and perfect is revealed. We are shown to all who can see that we are inadequate. It is like being stripped bare and your nakedness exposed to the public. Everyone can see you for who you are. All can see you in your weakness and frailty. The clothes of pretension that we cover ourselves in are stripped away and we stand just as we are, just as God has made us. The fear is that just as we are is not enough, just as we are is never enough, and we are ashamed. We are ashamed of who we are because we fear we are inadequate, and never enough.

But Adam and Eve were naked and felt no shame. They did not possess this feeling we call inadequacy. They did not feel like they were lacking. They did not feel like they didn't belong, or that they were not good enough, or that they were not loved and adored and valued. It was the opposite feelings that embraced them. Adam and Eve believed themselves to be adequate, to belong, to be worthy and important and loved. They had all the confidence in life and identity. They could stand naked, before each other and before God, and not feel ashamed.

This is the bliss of man in his native state. This is the

bliss of the young and naive. When we were children, we existed like our forebears. We did not think ourselves inadequate in any way, or that we were somehow deficient. There was no feeling of vulnerability that would cause us to feel exposed or under the judgment of others. We knew ourselves to be sufficient and to be worthy.

Perhaps it was an early moment on the playground that we felt the first hint that life might be different. Maybe when we were mocked or ridiculed for the clothes we wore or how we looked, or that we couldn't run as fast as the others or we were shorter than everyone else. For the first time, we were called out as being something other than sufficient and complete. We were made to feel small. Even worse, we were made to feel like we didn't matter. Perhaps, this is the beginning of that feeling called shame.

But as we were created, we did not possess that shame. There was no sense of vulnerability or inadequacy. There was instead a sense of acceptance and oneness with the whole world. The world was a safe place. It was a magical place. It was a place that invited us into it and embraced our entry. Life wanted us there and let us know how thrilled it was that we had become a part of it. There was nothing we had to hide or feel inadequate about.

This was life in the joy of innocence. The specter of shame had not touched us yet with its horrors of feeling small, inadequate and unworthy. We could be naked and not feel ashamed. We hardly even knew what it was to be naked at all. All life was wonder and joy, passion and intensity. We were confident in ourselves and our place in the world. And we had good reason to be.

In that original state we felt the delight of the universe. The world loved us and we could feel it. We were ultimately confident in who we were because we felt that delight. We felt the approval of creation. We felt it in the earth and the air, and even as the stars shone down at night. The world loved us, and we knew it. We were a part of the joy echoing through all the universe.

This is the world that Adam and Eve occupied in the garden. We are even told that it was the habit of the Lord to walk in the Garden in the cool of the evening. The Father was there with his children, he was close to them. His delight was upon them and they felt it. Life was a garden of goodness. This is all they knew.

We only have a brief time that we can live life on these terms, and that is only if we have a safe and happy childhood. It is only for a short time that we can feel that total trust and confidence in our environment. It is the paradise of living in the Father's abundance. As children, we ask and we receive. When we are hungry we are given food. When we cry we are given comfort. We are guarded by mother and father, tucked in, reassured, watched over, and provided for. We live in a garden as children, shielded from the horrors of the world.

How long we remain like this is different for each person. Some children are born to families that do not delight in their children, and the sense of wonder and innocence is lost quite early. Some are born into families of danger and harm. Their garden is a place of full of threats and evil, and they may hardly ever experience the sense that the universe delights in who they are. Some are sensitive souls, and they realize their separateness and inadequacy very early on. While others, either through a lack of awareness or great pride, hardly ever feel inadequate.

This is the world that initially was made for us all. We are made to exist in the delight of our heavenly Father. We are made to feel near to him, and feeling his love, know that we are important, that we are valued, that we are essential parts of his world. All of us are made to know that we belong. Confidence in life and in who God made us is our birthright. We are meant to know the love and delight of our Father, who delights truly in the children he made. We are made to live in his joy.

The great tragedy of the story of mankind is that this state does not remain. As it does not remain for us, it did not remain for our first parents. Innocence is lost, and with it the joy and the confidence of living. For when Adam and Eve first disobeyed, when they first sinned, first and most painful among the losses was that sense of joy, confidence, and delight in the Father. The tragedy we always focus on is the mortality, the death that came from disobedience. But the greater loss was losing the presence of the Father. For in losing that, what we really lost was the joy in living.

Part III

-

The Serpent

1 - Genesis 3:1-7

The Serpent

Now the serpent was more crafty than any other beast of the field that the Lord God had made.

He said to the woman, "Did God actually say, 'You shall not eat of any tree in the garden'?" And the woman said to the serpent, "We may eat of the fruit of the trees in the garden, but God said, 'You shall not eat of the fruit of the tree that is in the midst of the garden, neither shall you touch it, lest you die.'" But the serpent said to the woman, "You will not surely die. For God knows that when you eat of it your eyes will be opened, and you will be like God, knowing good and evil." So when the woman saw that the tree was good for food, and that it was a delight to the eyes, and that the tree was to be desired to make one wise, she took of its fruit and ate, and she also gave some to her husband who was with her, and he ate. Then the eyes of both were opened, and they knew that they were naked. And they sewed fig leaves together and made themselves loincloths.

The first animal we hear mentioned by name in the Bible is the serpent. Of all the creatures that God created, we are told the serpent is the craftiest. And this craftiness is not one that serves us well. With his guile, the serpent tempts Adam and Eve. He lies to them, telling them that the fruit that God has forbidden is not bad to eat. It is actually quite good. In fact, if Adam and Eve were to eat, they would be like God, knowing good and evil.

Much has been made of this serpent. We have speculated on who he is, and the consensus is that he is

Satan, the great tempter. The bigger question that many have asked is, How did he get there? If God is good, why did he make a creature that would tempt man to evil? Was he laying the seeds of our own destruction? Could God even create something evil? If not, then how did Satan become evil?

These questions are well beyond me and my intellectual capabilities. All I can glean from the existence of the serpent is to know that there is a force out there in the universe that wants to destroy me. There is a force out there that wants to see me fail. It wants me to self-destruct, commit evil acts, live selfishly, stagnate, remain immature and never reach my potential. There is a force out there that wants to see the worst in me come out and dominate that which is good in me. For me, that is enough to know, and that may be all I want or need to know.

If I am honest with myself, however, I must admit that the force of evil that works for my destruction is more than a cosmic force working outside of myself. Whatever the nature of this tempter may be, I find that there is within me a conspirator, one that works for the cause of tempter. There is a sinful, self-destructive streak that I nourish within my own heart. This is the part of me that desires not to do what is good but what is evil. It is the part of me that is selfish, angry, hateful, resentful, thinking only of myself and my own good. There may well be a cosmic force of evil that works to tempt and destroy mankind and all that is good, but this force of evil exists just as much a part of me and my own soul. There is a traitor in my own self, an impulse that works for its own destruction. The serpent lives inside of me.

It is not just me. A serpent lives in you as well, in all of us. We all walk around with that traitor within, an enemy within the walls of our hearts, who wants not goodness and blessing for us but desires that we be eaten alive by our own evil.

It is not a pleasant thought to consider, this traitor we may have inside. Many will deny it, not wanting to believe that evil may dwell in us. But if we are honest, we will admit we have been faced with moments when we did something we didn't want to do, or we felt overwhelmed by temptation, or we did something stupid and self-destructive. We probably looked back and had to ask ourselves why in the world we did such a thing. Very often we do not understand at all why we did them.

This, I believe, is the serpent working in us. It is a vile enemy that has lodged in our own hearts. It breathes out blasphemy and hate and wants us to indulge every evil impulse we possess. Even worse, it doesn't care whether we live or die. If we must be destroyed to carry out evil, then so be it.

This serpent we have, this part of us that conspires to do evil, is not all evil. Rather, it was not made for evil nor does it have to be evil. The serpent can actually be used for good. When we commit evil acts it may be under the influence and temptation of the serpent that we do so, but every act of the serpent within is not evil. We must remember that it is Jesus who tells us to be wise as serpents and gentle as doves.

The serpent, we are told, was the craftiest of the creatures that God had made. The serpent within us is made of that same quality. Our craftiness, our intelligence, our brains and our smarts—this is the serpent. In and of itself, it is not evil. It is good to be smart and wise. It is even good to be crafty.

Intelligence itself is good, but it is also through intelligence that we exercise that lowest of human qualities and highest of sins called pride. It is that place where we are strongest and weakest all at once. Remember, we are made in the image of God, and one of the ways that image is most manifest in us is through our intelligence, our reasoning. It is by our minds that we are like God and very different from any other animal in the world.

It is through the gift of intelligence that man is able to make his own decisions. Having his own intellect, his own thought process, he can look and evaluate the world on his own terms. He can look at something and form his own opinions about it. He does not have to take as fact what his mother and father told him about the world. He can look and think and make his own decisions about it. It is his right and ability to think for himself. This is a good quality that the serpent gives us. But it comes with a danger as well.

Adam and Eve were given a command, do not eat of the fruit from the tree of knowledge of good and evil, for it will kill you. Without a free intellect they could not think anything else but what had been told them. They would look at the fruit of the tree of knowledge, and see it as something evil, something that had to be avoided at all costs. But with a free and independent intellect they could come to other conclusions than the one told them by God. This is exactly what Eve did.

The Bible tells us that when *she saw* the fruit of the tree was good, and *she saw* that it was a delight and that it would make her wise, she ate. The emphasis is on the *she saw*. She evaluated the situation for herself. She was judging the tree for herself. She was no longer trusting in God's judgment. She was no longer assuming what God told her was right. What Eve was doing was looking at the situation brand new, not influenced at all by what God told her previously about the tree. She was deciding for herself if this fruit was good or not. She was trusting her own judgment over the word of God. The fruit looked good to her, and that was good enough.

What made Eve's action evil was not that she used her mind. What made it evil is that she trusted her mind, her own thoughts, her own intellect and evaluation of the situation rather than what was told her by the Lord. She trusted herself rather than trusting God. So the serpent, that part of us that is wise and clever, delivers us to our fall.

Trust in the self is the very cornerstone of pride. Some self-trust is good and even necessary. But to trust in the self over God is the pathway of sin and destruction, a mistake repeated billions of times a day. We look and decide for ourselves what is good and right.

Believe in yourself. Trust in yourself. Follow your heart. Follow your desires. These are the mantras we use to raise our young people. This is what we are feeding their souls. We believe we are teaching them confidence and self-esteem. What we are really teaching them is to commit the folly of Eve. Trust in your intellect rather than the word of God.

Because our intellect is that capacity to process information and think and reason, we must rely on it, every day. No one can go through life and not think for himself. In this respect the serpent is good. It is meant to guide us and direct us.

When the serpent goes evil is when we trust our intellect over God's wisdom. We are blessed with the intellect. We are blessed with the capacity to gain wisdom and learn. We are also vulnerable here. When we trust our own knowledge and insight over the word of God, we commit folly. We decide that we are wiser than God, that we know what is good and right. We believe we are the measure of all things and that, by our powers of thought, we can determine what is right and what is true. This is an awful abuse of the mind that God has given us.

The serpent can be a force of good. It all depends on

how we use our intellect. It should be taught to identify what is good and right rather than to think it can determine what is good and right. The mind should be taught to discern truth, not told that it gets to determine truth. The mind needs to begin with the truth that God has revealed to us and from that foundation begin to build the house of wisdom. Instead, we teach and encourage young minds to build their own foundations, forged from their own desires, and thus proceed to build a house of folly.

What the mind needs is humility. We need to learn with the realization that we are just creatures, not the creator. We need to learn that there is another who is greater than us, wiser than us, and whose ways are above us. We need to learn that man's wisdom, at its very best, will never compare even to God's folly. We need to learn that we are not the measure of all things, we are not the center of the universe, and this whole work of creation works to serve and glorify God. We are a part of that work, so what is proper for us is to work to glorify the God who made us.

This is the good for which the serpent was created. This is the proper use of our wisdom and intellect. We are to learn and gain wisdom and by it become the creation God made us to be. We are to use our minds to cultivate and keep the garden he gave us. We are to do it all to bring glory to God, and keep in mind that what is good for us is to trust in his ways. Trust in the ways of the Lord, and in all we do acknowledge him.

That man has an intellect is his first vulnerability, but it is by no means the only one that allowed his fall. Pride is something that usually is noted as the cause of disobedience. For good reason it is accused, for it is the pride of man that is the cause of the Fall more than any other.

To understand pride, though, is to understand the

114

nature of being made in the image of God. Made in his image means there is a glory within every human being. It is the glory of creatures made in the likeness of their creator. We all have this glory upon us, and with it comes a desire for more glory. Like intellect, this in itself is not a bad thing.

The idea of glory is often misunderstood. It is so wrapped up with pride that we think of glory as the desire to be elevated and praised above all things. Indeed, this is what it has become. But the Bible speaks of glory in very positive terms in many places, including man's glory[4]. There is no reason to think that human glory is a completely evil thing. It is the abuse of it that has led to evil.

Glory means having a certain honor or importance attached to us and to what we have done. Everyone wants this to some degree and even needs it. We want to have affirmation that our life is worthwhile. We want to know that we matter. We want to feel that our life has some significance to the grander scheme of the universe. We want to have weight and purpose.

Like intelligence, by nature this desire for glory is a positive attribute. But also like our intellectual capabilities, this good impulse carries a vulnerability. It is this desire for glory that makes us vulnerable to pride, a vice that seeks its glory by elevating the self over others, even God. As creatures made in the image of God, we were made to receive our glory from the Lord, but in pride, we seek it in the self.

As obedient children, who would follow his ways, work in his work, and look to lift up all he has done, we would properly find our glory. We would find our satisfaction

---

[4]Psalm 8:4-6, Psalm 30:11-12, Proverbs 16:31, Romans 2:6-11, 1 Corinthians 2:7, 2 Corinthians 3:18, 1 Peter 5:4

and our joy in glorifying him. When we recognize ourselves as his creatures, as his children (and children we will always be), then we seek our glory in his glory. This is how it is meant to work, and this way leads to glory to the one who would follow it.

But in pride we seek to glorify ourselves, not through glorifying God, but in directly lifting up the self. We do not wait to reflect his glory, we try to shine our own light. We do not magnify him, we magnify who we are. We don't strive to do his work but make every effort in getting people to recognize our work. This is the pride of the fallen. It seeks the glory of the self above the glory of others, even over the glory of God.

Adam and Eve, possessing this desire for glory, were vulnerable then to the temptations of the serpent. As the serpent without spoke, the serpent within them thrilled at the idea. You will become like God, they were promised. Inside them, their serpents, the crafty, intelligent, thinking part of themselves, loved the sound of that idea. We can have glory, they thought, all to ourselves. It will be all ours. We will owe our glory to no one and we will reflect no one. We will shine with the self. We will be like God.

Adam and Eve may have even thought that God might approve. They may have fooled themselves with this thinking. Won't our Father be proud, they may have said, when he sees us, looking like him, glorified like him, and done all by our own hand. Won't it be wonderful.

Ever since, man has warred for glory within himself and with every other person he meets. We still long to gain it by our own actions, to owe no one for our greatness. We still make that same mistake and think we are doing something good when we reach our hand out and take what looks good to our eyes and seems good to our minds.

The last feature of man that made him vulnerable to the fall was that essential fact of his nature that made disobedience possible in the first place—his free will.

There is a lot of confusion regarding the Fall and how it was made possible. If man was made good, as the scripture tells us, then how did he do something that was evil? His nature was good, created by God to be good. We believe or think that this should preclude him from doing anything evil.

Our misunderstanding, the source of our misunderstanding, is how we regard human nature. We have for so long become accustomed to treating man like all the other animals that we assume his nature is like the animals as well.

The other animals, we have come to understand, are creatures of instinct. Their nature is a fixed nature, of a sort. It is such that they will, or must, act a certain way when presented with certain stimuli. Their nature determines how they will act.

For example, a wolf pack will be led by an alpha, the strongest male wolf who will receive the preferences at feeding time. A buck will be drawn by the scent of a doe. The dog will walk in a circle before she lays down. A hen will respond to the sound of chicks in distress. Salmon will swim upstream to spawn.

Animals, we have decided, will pretty much allow their natures to rule over them and dictate their actions. They have no choice in this and must obey this nature. Humans can study them and even predict their behavior if we understand it. In fact, their instinct and nature has enabled us to train animals and evoke responses in them by manipulating this nature.

Man has been supposed to be in the same lot as the animals. Albeit a more complicated animal, he is still considered just an animal and his nature similar to the other beasts. He has a fixed nature, and if we were to understand it completely, it could be manipulated like the other animals. This theory has gained such ascendancy among intellectuals that humanity is largely regarded as not possessing any free will at all. Man is assumed more and more to be just another animal that is ruled over by instincts and desires, helpless against the nature that directs even his thoughts.

Because there is certainly an animal part to man's nature, there is also a part that responds to stimuli in the same way that animals do, in a fairly predictable fashion. But that is not all there is to man. Human beings also possess the image of the Spirit of God. His spirit is free.

What we need to understand about the nature of humanity, is that this nature is free. We possess a free will nature. That is our true nature. Because our nature is free, we have to consider it and understand that nature in a very different way than any other creature of the earth.

In some ways, we cannot even talk about the nature of man. The very idea of man having a nature excludes the possibility of him being free. Having a nature implies a certain program or way in which he will tend to act. We may see this from time to time, but we also see human beings acting in very different and unpredictable ways. We see that no two people respond to circumstances in the same way. We see children raised in the same home grow to be very different kinds of adults. We see many victims of evil decide to be good. And we see children raised in good homes grow up to be monsters. In essence, there is no law or fixed nature when it comes to man.

Because human beings are free will creatures it is useless to talk about his nature. His nature is free, which means his nature will be what he decides it will be. Even if he is made good, he can decide to be evil. Even if he is made evil, or subjected to evil, he can decide to be good.

Of course, all humans have tendencies that are subject to fairly predictable outcomes. A child of an alcoholic has a good chance of becoming an alcoholic. The child of an abuser will more likely abuse others. Kids raised in houses of evil, that have had evil done to them, will more likely be evil themselves one day. But they also may not. That's just it about human beings. You never know exactly how one will turn out. His behavior can never be fully predicted.

This means that no matter what the circumstance, man is free to decide. He doesn't have to do this or that. He may be compelled or tempted to act a certain way, but he doesn't have to. Nothing binds him to one form of behavior or thought. He can do what he wants to do. He can even want what he wants to want. There is no necessity or "have to" in his nature.

This is why the question, is man born good or evil, is a useless question. Man was made good. Because of the Fall his nature is corrupted (more on this later), but he is also free. This means his nature is designed as an open and fluid nature. It is yet to be determined, still in the process of formation.

Human nature is free, and because of this, we see that no guilt can be impugned to God for what happened at the Fall. He did not make Adam to fail. The man and woman were made good, but they used their free will to do that which was evil. It was their choice, or rather the exercise of that choice, that led to the Fall.

The composition of man, which is both good and glorious, also carries all the vulnerabilities that led to his fall. His intellect which can assess a situation and think for itself; his pride, which desires a glory all on its own; his will, which allows him to act according to his own will and not according to a predetermined nature—all these together combine to make the human creature vulnerable to temptation. The serpent only exploited this weakness.

It used the serpent within, through which we were already vulnerable to temptation. It is not that a part of us is evil, but it can be tempted to evil. The intellect is good, but can tend to rely on its own thoughts and outlooks over the command of God. The desire for glory is one that can draw us towards God or set us up as enemies to God. The will, by which we choose, can lead us to acts of great nobility and virtue, or we can choose that which is base and evil. The serpent within can serve God, or it can seek to serve itself. The serpent of the garden did not make us commit evil. It only twisted the serpent within us to choose the desire of the heart over the will of God.

This leads us to a final question: If God knew that we would fall if he made our natures free, then why did he give us free natures? Would it not have been better to give us good natures, so that we would not have been able to fall, and would be enjoying paradise to this day? Evil would never have touched the world.

True, the Lord has chosen to make us free rather than good, and this is the root of all the evil in the world. By making us free, he made evil an choice. It is a choice God must have known we would make.

But what kind of creatures would we be if God gave us a fixed nature? Certainly we would be nothing like what we call human. We would do only that which is good, but could we really call it good if we had no choice but to act that way? We never talk about animals as being good or evil, even when they do something as appalling as savaging their own young. They only act according to their nature. To be truly good, to be able to say that you acted for good, implies a choice. If we must act good then you cannot say that any act we carry out is good. Only if one chooses to do good can you really say that he is good.

To be made without a free will is to be made an automaton, like a robot, merely slaves to our programing.

This may sound tempting to some, for that would take all evil out of the world. But it makes us less than human. It is the temptation of every utopia to force people to do what is good, make them behave properly. But this is a temptation to take away the most precious gift we humans possess—our freedom. Only by that freedom can we truly be good. Good can never be forced or compelled. Goodness must be a choice, or it cannot be good at all.

This is a lesson our politicians would do well to heed, especially toady, as ideas begin to circulate desiring a more perfect society in America instead of the free society that it was designed to be. No nation on earth will ever be without problems. Evil cannot be legislated out or educated away. Any regime or government that seeks to impose too absolutely an ideal society will always end up carrying out atrocities that are much worse than the original evil they were trying to eradicate. Utopianism will always fail.

We know it will fail because the only utopia man ever lived in failed. It was not because of God's poor design that the Garden failed. It failed because of God's love. His love is such that he would make us free, allow us to be ourselves, even if that freedom threatens the purity of his design. He does not force us to be a certain way because he loves us. And in all true love, the beloved must be as he will be, not forced to be a certain way. Because God loves us, he wants us to be like him. Because of that same love, he waits for us to choose to be like him. He will not force but teach. He will not compel but show. And he will not deprive us of choice, even knowing that we may choose evil. It is not the mystery of God's will that allows this, that we must marvel and wonder on. This is the mystery of his love, one that remains active and strong, even as we use the choice he has given us to destroy what he has made.

2 - Genesis 3:8-13

The Fall

And they heard the sound of the Lord God walking in the garden in the cool of the day, and the man and his wife hid themselves from the presence of the Lord God among the trees of the garden. But the Lord God called to the man and said to him, "Where are you?" And he said, "I heard the sound of you in the garden, and I was afraid, because I was naked, and I hid myself." He said, "Who told you that you were naked? Have you eaten of the tree of which I commanded you not to eat?" The man said, "The woman whom you gave to be with me, she gave me fruit of the tree, and I ate." Then the Lord God said to the woman, "What is this that you have done?" The woman said, "The serpent deceived me, and I ate."

When we talk about the Fall, what do we mean? Where did man fall from? Where did he fall to? It wasn't a geographic event, for we did not plummet from a great height to a lower one. Nor could it be said that Adam and Eve occupied heaven and after the Fall were cast down to earth. What was the Fall exactly?

When Adam and Eve fell, they fell from a place of glory and grace. They fell in favor. It was not the loss of their state of ease and pleasure that made the Fall what it was. What Adam and Eve lost in the moment of their fall was that sense of confidence and security that naturally belonged to them in the Garden.

In this sense the greatest consequence of the Fall was a

psychological one. All that followed the Fall, of which we will talk later, the greatest was spiritual devastation. Many of the other consequences that follow can themselves be traced back to this mental state that humanity now occupies.

It was noted earlier that in the Garden Adam and Eve were naked and were not ashamed. We understand that they could do this because they were blessed by God with a sense of confidence and peace in who they were.

This was the true state of blessing occupied by our original mother and father. Like children who knew they were adored by their father, Adam and Eve lived with the delight of God. They knew they were accepted by and approved by him. They knew without a doubt that God loved them and treasured their existence, that they were considered the greatest and most precious thing that the Lord God made. How wonderful an existence that must have been. It was to exist like happy children.

When man first ate of that fruit forbidden by God, when he did what was not permitted, the first thing that happened to him was that he felt shame. The Fall was immediate. He did not have to wait for God to discover the sin, for he felt immediately within him that something had changed.

As soon as he ate the fruit that promised to make him like God, he could see at once the stark truth: he was not God. What he saw, now knowing good and evil, was that he had done something evil. He had disobeyed the will of the Father. He could likely see that any semblance he shared with God, that divine image of the Father, was immediately tarnished by what he had done.

It is that same desire that led us to disobedience that leads us to feel the sense of shame at our fall. Pride is the root of both. Pride is what led to the Fall, and it is that same pride that instills in us a sense of shame. For it was the desire for glory, not the glory given us by God, but the desire for the glory of God himself, that lead us first to disobedience (and leads us still). It was also that pride that made us feel ashamed at who we are (and it also does it today).

For what else is shame other than this sense that we are inadequate, and we don't measure up to others? Shame is when we feel small, vulnerable, unworthy, unloved, exposed for being who we should not. To feel this way we first create a sense of who we should be or who we want to be. As soon as we discover we are not that person, we become vulnerable to shame, for then we can see ourselves as being inadequate.

Adam set himself up to be God. As soon as he ate of the forbidden fruit, his eyes were open. He found out that he was not only less than God, but he was suddenly less than Adam. We feel shame for the same reason. We know ourselves as less than God, but also poor versions of ourselves. The main reason it is shameful for us is that we have set ourselves up as being a lofty creature, someone who is good, beautiful and wonderful. Like Adam, we reach out to be like God. And it is when we find that we are not God, but simple creatures that have been made, creatures of the dust and earth, we feel our smallness and our inadequacy so powerfully that it manifests as shame. Suddenly is gone our sense of confidence and peace, our oneness with the world, our certainty that we are loved and treasured. This is what it means to fall.

Awareness can be a wonderful thing, but it also comes with dangers. Through awareness we can feel that sense of vulnerability and inadequacy. We see ourselves as separate from everyone else, alone. We are not like the others, who are all a part of that whole called "everyone else." We alone are not a part of that. This increases our sense of vulnerability, our shame. What we do, then, is present another face to the world. This way they do not know who we really are. We can hide our inadequacy and the terrible fact that we, unlike everyone else around us, are a fallen and unworthy creature.

That is why man, alone of all the other animals, wears clothes. He alone sees himself as an independent creature, not truly part of the whole, but not really apart from it either. He alone feels this vulnerability called shame. We, like Adam and Eve, are compelled to cover up those faults, that basic humanness, and make for ourselves clothes to cover up our nakedness. I was afraid, Adam tells God when he is caught, because I was naked. He had not been afraid before. He was only afraid then because he knew himself as naked. He knew himself as a creature who bore guilt. His confidence and glory had deserted him, and he knew only himself as a pitiful creature who had disobeyed God. So he covered himself.

We cover ourselves for the same reason. We are afraid, for we know ourselves as naked. We are afraid that other people will see us for who we are. We will be found out as unworthy and not fit to belong. So we wear clothes. But we wear them not only on our bodies but on our minds as well. We wear disguises and coverings of all types, lest anyone see who we really are and know the awful truth.

The only exception to this would be people who for some reason possess so little self-awareness as to not feel shame (which may be the result of some handicap or dementia) and those who are arrogant enough to never see themselves as inadequate. These are the people who think so highly of themselves, or who have never looked too deeply into themselves as to not be able to feel shame at all. For they are still under the deception that they are gods. And though we marvel at them for their confidence, it is a confidence of illusion. For if their arrogance is not stripped away by life, and lead to repentance, then it will be stripped away by God, and lead to a far worse fate.

Much of what we do in life is a quest to restore this sense of confidence and glory that rightfully belongs to us. We search for that sense of peace and acceptance that we enjoyed in the Garden. The world tells us we can get it back by one great accomplishment or another. The world tells us if we can make enough money, or achieve this or that great thing, then it will restore to us that lost light. But none of these things work. We all fail at restoring our glory because none of what the world can give can restore that which is a gift of heaven. Pleasure fails because we can never have enough. Money fails because there is always more to be made. Power and fame can be fickle and as difficult to maintain as it was to achieve.

Perhaps the most worthless way of restoring our lost confidence is that universal advice of our age to believe in yourself. That is what we are told. Believe in yourself. That's all you have to do, and you will be strong, confident and happy. Believe in yourself and you will have peace.

In truth, nothing could be more wrong. "Believe in yourself" is the worst piece of advice anyone can give you. It is a hateful and odious saying, almost as stupid as it is wrong. Believing in yourself will not bring you peace and confidence. To believe in yourself is only to mire yourself in the trap that originally put you, put us, in this bind in the first place. For it was Eve, believing in herself, that led to the Fall originally. And it is believing in the self, over and above the word of God, that perpetuates the sin and shame of our world.

It is our self that is the problem; our self, fallen and dejected, that caused our inadequacies in the first place. How can believing in this miserable self accomplish anything at all? This advice only asks us to ignore the sense of inadequacy that we all feel. It only inflates a pride that is our destruction. And if we know ourselves to be

126

inadequate and worthy of shame, how does believing in that fallen and inadequate self suddenly and magically cure our ills? It only covers up the problem with denial. It is this mantra, repeated by many well meaning mouths, that has fueled the epidemic of narcissism and arrogance that has taken over our culture. At the same time, it fuels the outbreak of the loneliness and depression that has also become rife in our world today. For as much as we try to believe in ourselves, to build ourselves up, to make ourselves out to be something wonderful and grand, our denial can only carry us so far. Despite what we tell ourselves, we know deep down that we are really fallen and inadequate creatures. No amount of self-affirmation can change this.

The only way to reclaim what was lost is not through more pride but in humility. It is in humility that we see ourselves not as these great, powerful and wonderful things but as mere creatures. It is in humility that we remind ourselves that we are not God, but only human. This is the road back to peace with God and peace with ourselves. This is the road where we find our confidence again in life and feel the love of the Father.

When faced with our sin, humility tells us to confess and repent. Pride tells us to hide our sin, make excuses, justify, or blame someone else. This is exactly what Adam and Eve do. Neither one takes accountability for their actions, but they blame someone else. Adam blames Eve. Eve blames the serpent. Adam goes further and even puts the blame on God. The woman you gave me, he says, told me to eat the fruit. See, it is your fault, God, because you gave me this woman. Look what she made me do.

We always prefer to put our problems on other people. We are eager to do so. It is another way of wearing clothes, hiding our flaws and weaknesses from the world. It is a reaction of fear, born of inadequacy. We lack the courage and fortitude to shoulder the blame ourselves. For to admit our blame and fault is to expose our nakedness. So, we blame others.

Who was to blame for our failing? Who is at fault in that original of all sins? There is certainly blame to go around.

No one took blame for what happened, but all are at fault. The serpent is to blame for his tempting. The woman is to blame for accepting. Adam is to blame for going along with it all. Anybody except God can honestly accept culpability for what happened. But none of them accepted it.

This is the gut reaction today of all the descendants of Adam and Eve. When we are confronted with a problem, or caught doing something we should not have, we blame others. It is always someone else's fault, it is never our own. It is the fault of the Devil. It is the fault of society. It is the fault of our circumstances. It is politics, or the rich, or the media, or even our natures. It is the fault of the bartender who served me the drinks, says the drunk driver who kills a family of four, not my fault who decided to drink in the first place. And we let them get away with it. We even continue to blame God. For it is God who made us like we are. It is God who made the world like it is. And even more, it is God who has the power to stop whatever it is that is going wrong. It is the fault of anyone but ourselves.

What we don't do is admit that our problems, our failings, and our sins are our own. What we don't do is admit that they are our own fault and of our own doing. As long as we try to dodge responsibility for our sins and failings, they will never get solved and they will never get better. Our sins will always haunt us as long as we blame others rather than take ownership ourselves.

Adam lost paradise. First, he lost it for disobedience,

for a prideful disobedience that trusted his own desire over the word of God. He believed in himself more than he believed in God. Then, he compounded this sin by refusing to admit his guilt and simply confess his sin and ask for the mercy of God.

I wonder if this second sin had as much to do with losing paradise as the first one did. I often wonder if Adam could not have regained the Garden, in at least some form, by owning up to his sin, by confessing his fault and taking the blame. God is always one to show mercy to those who repent. I believe he would have shown some to Adam had our forefather had the courage and humility to ask for it.

But Adam did not ask for forgiveness. He did not confess his faults. He took the cowardly, prideful road and blamed others for his failings. He even blamed God.

As with other behaviors, Adam is our model. As he acted, so we tend to act. Just as he never overcame his failings by ignoring them, we will never overcome our problems as long as we try to blame others. We will only compound our issues that way.

It is only by admitting the role we play in our failings and shortcomings, by admitting that these sins are our fault and our fault alone, that we can have any hope of rising above and beyond them. It is only through humility, and the repentance that comes out of humility, that we can become better than our failings.

Our tendency remains to deny and to blame. This is as universal a trait as there is among people. It is almost so reliable as to be a guarantee. When faced with our sins, we will deny and blame others.

Both our sin and our denial of sin is due to pride. We trust first in ourselves, seek to glorify ourselves, following our own way instead of the way of God, and this leads us to sin. Then, when faced with our sins, our pride tells us to hide them, deny them, and blame others. We acted this way at the outset of our very first sin, and we act this way for all of them. This is how we lost paradise, and this is how it remains lost to us today.

3 - Genesis 3:14-19

Consequences of the Fall

The Lord God said to the serpent,

"Because you have done this,
cursed are you above all livestock
and above all beasts of the field;
on your belly you shall go,
and dust you shall eat
all the days of your life.
I will put enmity between you
and the woman,
and between your offspring and
her offspring;
he shall bruise your head,
and you shall bruise his heel."

To the woman he said,

"I will surely multiply your pain in
childbearing;
in pain you shall bring forth children.
Your desire shall be contrary to your
husband,
but he shall rule over you."

And to Adam he said,

"Because you have listened to the voice of your
wife and have eaten of the tree of which I
commanded you, 'You shall not eat of it,'

cursed is the ground because of you;
in pain you shall eat of it all the days

of your life;
thorns and thistles it shall bring
forth for you;
and you shall eat the plants of the field.
By the sweat of your face
you shall eat bread,
till you return to the ground,
for out of it you were taken;
for you are dust,
and to dust you shall return."

Despite their attempts to escape guilt, all the creatures involved in the original disobedience are cursed. The Fall will have its consequences that will touch not only the nature of man, but all of nature. What once was a garden paradise will become the troubled earth we know and live in today.

The first one cursed is the serpent. He will be forced to slither upon the ground and eat dust. Furthermore, there will be war and enmity between the children of Eve and the serpent. He will bite the heel of her offspring, and they will crush his head.

Two things can be understood by this. For one, mankind now has an enemy. We could say we have two enemies, but they are both serpent. There is the serpent within and the serpent without.

The serpent outside of us is the most familiar. This is the spiritual enemy that people refer to as the devil or Satan. After the curse, his existence will be a bane to ours. From now on we have a spiritual enemy, a powerful force in the heavenly realms that desires our destruction. He will torment and tempt us. He will stoke the evil side of us and then accuse us of what he has led us to do. He will work for our destruction and our downfall. And he will hate when we succeed and do good. This is the reality for human beings - a spiritual enemy working against us.

As a result of the curse, the serpent within us, our intelligence and desire for glory that has turned to pride, is our greatest enemy. Far more sinister than the spiritual tempter, the greatest danger we face is the desire that we carry within our own hearts. And even though it is a part of us, it is also an enemy. It is a traitor that, desiring its own exaltation above anything else, will drive the self to death if necessary. Between glorifying God and enjoying life, or glorifying the self and suffering death, the serpent is quite ready to choose death. For nothing is as loathsome for the serpent within us than to glorify anything else, even God. It is the self or nothing.

This pride, this serpent within, is brought low as well. Just as the outer serpent was cursed to slither on the ground, the inner serpent is made to do the same. Our pride is brought low. Forever after it will feel inadequate and small. It will be driven by a need to elevate and lift itself up. It will always need attention and praise. It will be obsessed with its own glory. Because the serpent knows it is low, it will work tirelessly to convince itself and others that it is high and glorious.

For Eve, there are two parts to her curse. First, she will have pain in childbirth. We can rightly assume from this that had it not been for their disobedience, then delivering babies would be an easier affair. But now it will be difficult.

Though women may not feel it as acutely due to medical advances, this was a terrible curse in the centuries leading up to our own. Childbirth was dangerous for women and caused the death of thousands. Even if childbirth didn't result in death, the complications of pregnancy and delivery were very common causes of female mortality. What could have been easy for the body now became a burden. At the same time, the desire to have children, the biological urge of the body to reproduce did not diminish. Something that is a danger to the woman's body is also something that her body would desire.

The other part of the curse is that the woman will have a desire for her husband, and that her husband will rule over her. It is possible that originally Adam and Eve shared an egalitarian relationship, but as she was the first tempted and fell prey to the words of the serpent and her desire, she bears a curse to be under her husband.

Despite what changes our society has tried to enact to reverse this, it still remains a natural tendency among couples, not all, but most will tend toward the husband to have authority in the family. And while the protest today is that this state of affairs is social convention that can easily be undone, we are told in scripture that this is a result of the curse. The unspoken difficulty our culture faces in trying to right this is that we struggle against the curse that God has laid on the man and woman. It is more than social convention at work here.

Compounding this difficulty is the change in nature that came about as a result of the curse. It says that the woman's desire will be for her husband. This is now written in the fabric of the female soul; her desire will be for the approval of men.

It has been a readily observed fact that many, if not most, women will seek approval and satisfaction in life through their relationships. This is how they often find a sense of worth, approval, and value. To have broken and failed relationships is a sign for many women that their life is damaged and worthless. Among relationships, the married relationship is usually the most important. This signals success more than any other. It is of deep significance for women to have a husband. It exists for men, but not in the same way. A man who struggles to find a wife will not internalize feelings of unworth the same way a woman who cannot get married will. Struggles to find a spouse do not strike men as acutely as they do women. As much as some would like to blame society for this, I suspect we need look no further than the curse laid upon us. When we see women doing so much for the approval of men, when we decry the unfair standards of beauty, when we complain of the competition that women have with one another, our blame needs to go to the curse, to the scourge of human sin, the result of our pride, and the serpent within that seeks to destroy us.

For the man, his punishment is work. Rather, it is that his work will no longer be a work of ease. It is said that by his sweat he will bring forth bread out of the ground, and the ground will yield for him thorns and thistles.

Before this, the work of man was an easy work. All that was required of him was to cultivate and keep the garden that God had already made. And the circumstances made it easier. The trees gave their fruit freely and required little labor. Because God's blessing was so powerfully upon Adam, all that he set out to do certainly succeeded. He hardly ever met with failure or found any of his tasks too difficult to accomplish. This would not be anymore.

The work that man was commanded to do from the beginning was to continue. This was the work of maintaining what God had made. But now this work would be labor. The ground, which always gave abundantly, would give only grudgingly. It would take effort to do anything, and failure was always a certainty. That which was easy would become hard. It would only be through sweat and effort that Adam could hope for success.

We see a change, then, not just in the man and woman, but in all of nature and their relationship to the world around them. The man and woman are cursed, but so is the ground cursed because of them. Because of the authority the man and woman possessed—keepers of the earth—as it went with them it would go with the whole world. Because they were cursed, the earth would also feel the curse.

This is the root of what we call natural evil. Plagues, disease, famine, natural disaster, tornado, flood. All sorts of evils that we mistake for natural occurrences are also attributable to the Fall. The earth has turned against us as surely as we have turned against God. Man's reign over the earth is broken.

Because of our position as stewards of the earth, we were in that unique position to affect the fortunes of the entire planet with our behavior. All evil then, even what we call natural evil, comes back to the foot of man to blame. We are the cause of the natural as well as the human evil. This is as true today as when it first happened.

Just as the woman has a desire for her husband, so the man will be plagued by a desire to achieve through his work. Both the man and the woman have lost their confidence in life, because they have been cut off from the source of their peace and their happiness. What we know is fear and uncertainty, the feelings of inadequacy and alienation. It is our deep ambition to fill that void left behind by the departed presence of God. We attempt to fill it with work, or relationships, or pleasure, power or wealth. All these attempts assuredly fail. These things will not fill the emptiness inside. The hunger still rages in us, so we allow ourselves to be driven by ambition. We tell ourselves it is only ambition to accomplish, or do great things, or make a name for ourselves, or make a difference in the world. But the reality is that our ambition is an attempt to fill the void that exists in the heart of every man and woman. We are empty. We are no longer filled with the presence and blessing of our Father. We feel lost and empty and incomplete, and all the passion and joy is drained from life. This is the true cost of the curse.

This is how we exist today as such driven people. We are always looking and never satisfied. Much of the work of civilization, both as individuals and as groups, is due to this feeling of inadequacy. The whole of modern civilization is built by this fear.

All of us have become driven in some way. We feel this insatiable need to grasp or achieve, or do anything that we can to elevate ourselves because we lack that mature conviction which should be ours by nature. Without it, we are afraid. We yearn for that affirmation that we are an important piece in the created order. We long for that sense of belonging that will assure us we are accepted. We hunger for that lost day, even if our conscious mind does not remember, when we trusted in God and believed in the inherent goodness of life.

Instead we have none of these things. All we are left with is a sense of our own nakedness.

This is the true depth and misery of the curse. We are separated and alienated from the presence of God. In that alienation comes the fear and insecurity that drives us.

What we truly desire is to feel like children again. We want to feel like children of God. We want to be confident that God is not just watching over us but that he loves us and desires our good. We want to be confident again that we are valued and accepted by our Father.

If we were to feel the delight of the Father again, we could be free from our fear and insecurity. This is the only way to be free from it, because then we return to its true source. Alienation from the Father is our great psychological curse and burden. Healing that relationship is the only cure. The failure of the modern self-help movement highlights this problem. No amount of self-affirmation can undo what the curse has laid upon us. We cannot talk ourselves out of our misery. We can only conquer this fear and insecurity by seeking the love of the Father.

This is the great journey of the psyche. This is the quest of the modern, alienated soul. To regain what was lost is everything. We cannot regain the Garden again, but we may regain some of the confidence that was torn from us, the confidence that we are treasured, valued, and loved. If we would be able to do this, then life on earth would become markedly different.

For once, we would be free from fear and insecurity. Being thus free we would no longer be driven by these self-deprecating emotions. We would become expansive and large. We would feel the delight of the Father, and feeling that delight, be capable of acting under impulses other than fear. Something other than naked ambition fostered by terror would become the force of human civilization. We could be driven by passion, by love, by genuine affection for God and for one another. Imagine the world we could build, if this passion, rather than fear, was the driving force behind our life.

4 - Genesis 3:20-24

Death Comes

The man called his wife's name Eve, because she was the mother of all living. And the Lord God made for Adam and for his wife garments of skins and clothed them.

Then the Lord God said, "Behold, the man has become like one of us in knowing good and evil. Now, lest he reach out his hand and take also of the tree of life and eat, and live forever—" therefore the Lord God sent him out from the garden of Eden to work the ground from which he was taken. He drove out the man, and at the east of the garden of Eden he placed the cherubim and a flaming sword that turned every way to guard the way to the tree of life.

The Lord concedes to the new state that Adam and Eve occupy. They know they are naked and will not tolerate this any longer. So the Lord makes them clothes, and from here on out clothing and covering will become a necessity for the man and woman. They are aware now. With awareness, nakedness cannot be tolerated.

At this point God turns and speaks to others present with him. We have not been introduced to any of these other beings, nor is it said who they are. Some have said that they are other gods or angels that the Lord speaks with. Some say it is the Trinity. Many scholars have simply called this group the divine council and left it there. The fact is, we don't know who the "us" is that God refers to.

Whoever it is, God turns to them and says that man has become "like one of us." Something is different with the young humans. They are not the same creatures they were before. Though they were originally made in the image of God, now they are even more like God.

The difference is that man now has awareness. There has grown in him an expansion of consciousness that was not originally intended for him. Specifically, he has gained knowledge of good and evil. Now, he is like the divine creatures that the Lord God is speaking to. He knows the difference between good and evil. He has become a moral creature.

It is hard for us to understand why this would be considered a bad thing at all. Knowing good and evil is considered good, a sign of maturity and wisdom. Men are supposed to know the difference between good and evil and even work to know the difference better.

It is true that for us to know good and evil, and be able to distinguish between the two is, in fact, good. But if we remained in a state where we did not know the difference, we would maintain a state of innocence. And if we were in innocence, not knowing good and evil, then we would never incur guilt for what we may have done wrong. Not knowing the difference, good and evil would not exist for us. We would be incapable of doing evil. Even if we did something that today would be considered evil, it would not have been evil for us. Not knowing the difference, we could not bear guilt.

But as soon as we ate of the fruit of the knowledge of good and evil, our innocence was lost. We could no longer act and claim that we did not know any better. We know better now. We are liable to guilt.

But something seems more pressing for God and the beings that he is addressing. He not only observes that man has become like them, knowing good and evil, but shows worry that man also might stretch out his hand, take from the tree of life, and live forever.

This seems to be the main concern of the Lord. Now that they have eaten of knowledge, that they know good and evil, they might take hold of the tree of life and eat of that, too. If they were to do that, then they would really be like gods, living forever.

The story has in it a sort of heartbreaking suspense. If only we had known sooner. If only we had not chosen the tree of knowledge first. How close eternal life was for man, and we let it slip through our fingers.

We are told that the tree of life was in the garden the entire time. It was mentioned at the beginning, but it did not seem to present a temptation like the tree of knowledge did. I often wonder why this was. Why did the fruit of knowledge look so appealing and the fruit of life did not? Was there something unsightly about the tree? Did the fruit appear bitter? For some reason they were not drawn to or tempted by that fruit.

I can only suppose what may have been the reason. And it may have been, that in their innocence, Adam and Eve knew nothing of death. They already possessed life, so they felt no need to acquire it. Not knowing of death, and being like children, they supposed that life would continue like it was forever. They would have had no conception of the end of things, least of all their own lives.

But when they ate of the tree of knowledge, one of the things they discovered was that they were mortal creatures. They made that awful realization that they would one day perish, and like all flesh return to the dust from which they came. When man took hold of knowledge, he also took hold of that most terrifying secret of life—that we would die.

It should come as no surprise that insecurity rose in us with such force and terror. It should not surprise us that fear and uncertainty became a prime feature of man. We discovered we were such weak and vulnerable creatures.

In one respect, we are like God, different from the animals, upright and noble and beautiful, masters of the world. But fools we are to think that we are too much like God. This poor casing of flesh will get old and rot, decay and return to the dust from which it came.

In the book of Psalms we are told, "Teach us to number our days that we may gain a heart of wisdom."[5] There is a clear link made between wisdom and awareness of our own death. So it would not be that great of an assumption to believe that when Adam ate of the knowledge of good and evil, and when his eyes were opened, the shock that made his eyes go wide was the sudden and horrifying realization that he was a mortal creature. For the first time he knew he was going to die. Being the first to gain that knowledge, Adam and Eve became the first to learn the perilous cost of wisdom.

I only speculate here, but I wonder if it was God's plan at some point for Adam and Eve to eat of both the tree of knowledge and of life. I wonder if it was only forbidden for a time. Perhaps there was some method or process in the development of the fledgling humans. When the time was right they would be given both knowledge and life.

This is something we can never rightly know. Whatever was to happen in the Garden, the chance was lost, and God was not going to let us eat and live forever. Being in a state of sin, if we were to eat of the tree of life, we would not only be sinful and fallen creatures, but also living forever in sin. To deny man the tree of life at this point was a mercy. It would not be well for man, or the rest of creation, to be immortal and fallen. Whatever time line God had planned for us was ruined, and life was denied for us except the few short years we have on earth, occupying bodies of dust.

---

[5]Psalm 90:12

142

The full brunt of the curse falls upon the man and woman. They are dust, and to dust they will inevitably return. They are mortal, and mortal we shall remain, tasting of death. The way of all flesh is our way, too. We will all die.

This has become an irrevocable fact of life. We will die. I will die. You will die. We are all doomed to that fate called mortality. It will be a fate that doesn't just touch us, it touches everything we experience and encounter. This earth is a place where death reigns.

Here we encounter the great sorrow of man. It is not just that we will die, but everything we touch, all that we accomplish, all that we do will also one day pass from the earth and be no more. Even those who achieve their loftiest ambitions will one day have their accomplishments taken from the world.

In Percy Shelley's poem, *Ozymandias*, he tells the story of a mighty pharaoh who made the whole world tremble beneath his power. He built great monuments to himself so that he might be remembered forever. Today, those monuments lay buried in the sand, with shepherds resting their backs on the half-exposed faces. He who was once the terror of the world has been forgotten and his monuments for eternity reduced to a back rest for shepherds. It is not just our bodies that die—our names will die too.

When death was brought into the world, an eternal change was also invited in. It ensures that we don't just die but are forgotten also. The young will grow old. Legends will fade. We may have our day in the sun, then it is back to the shade. One day, stories about us will no longer be told. The writing on our tombstone will fade away, but that is long after people no longer visit the site where we are buried.

It is a depressing thought for many. For others it is

terrifying. And for some it means all of life is futile. But this is the heart of wisdom. We are not supposed to be here forever. We are not meant to always walk and occupy this tortured earth. Life is a passage, not a place. This is the realm of a journey, a transition, not a world where we can make a permanent home.

This certainty, this irrevocable fact of life, should be the starting place and cornerstone of every philosophy or outlook on life. It's not just that we die, but that even the memory of who we are and what we did will die, our memories gone and our achievements forgotten. This should serve as the basis for any worldview or ethic we might build. In all things, we should consider our mortality, and remember the mortality of all that we do.

To do this makes life all at once a very serious and a very comical affair. It is at the same time something dreadful and irresistibly hilarious. Life, we find, has a great weight to it, but also a great levity.

Life is weighty and serious because it is so brief. We only have a short moment here on the earth. Once our years have passed, the opportunity is gone forever. We should make the very most of our fleeting moments. To make the most requires great seriousness, so we do not squander a single breath. Life should be taken very seriously.

At the same time, there is an impossible levity to life. It is almost comical. It doesn't matter what we do, how hard we work, how serious we are about achieving our ambition. It will all die and fade. The hardest working and the laziest on earth share the same fate. Our ambition will lead us one day to obscurity. All that we do will have no impact on the world 100, 200, 1000 years from now. Let us, then, not take life too seriously. We should eat, drink and be merry, for tomorrow we die.

And so we find ourselves in this place that is solemn as

144

death, and as comical as the grave. Life is a serious affair, yet we should not take ourselves too seriously.

Everything dies. Time moves on whether we like it or not, whether we are ready for it or not. We have no choice in the matter, just as we had no choice to be born into the world. What passes on can never return. The past is gone and youth will never be reclaimed from the theft of time. There is a sorrow to this knowledge, but it comes with a profound beauty that can hardly be expressed in words.

Adam and Eve were evicted from the Garden. The Lord posted an angel to guard the way, equipped with a flaming sword. That path was barred forever. There was no going back, for them or for us.

The way to our paradise, whether the real one or the one we occupied as children when the world seemed to us a garden of delight, is taken from us and the way barred forever. We cannot go back and reverse what happened. We cannot return to the Garden. Any attempts on our part to reclaim what was lost are futile at best.

Our destiny now lies forward, along the march of time. Our destiny lies before us, along the passage of life. We can no more look behind, for we have been cast out of the Garden and into the land to work our way through life. And the way never goes back. This is our destiny now.

Life only moves forward. This too, is good.

5 - Genesis 4:1-16

Murder

Now Adam knew Eve his wife, and she conceived and bore Cain, saying, "I have gotten a man with the help of the Lord." And again, she bore his brother Abel. Now Abel was a keeper of sheep, and Cain a worker of the ground. In the course of time Cain brought to the Lord an offering of the fruit of the ground, and Abel also brought of the firstborn of his flock and of their fat portions. And the Lord had regard for Abel and his offering, but for Cain and his offering he had no regard. So Cain was very angry, and his face fell. The Lord said to Cain, "Why are you angry, and why has your face fallen? If you do well, will you not be accepted? And if you do not do well, sin is crouching at the door. Its desire is contrary to you, but you must rule over it."

Cain spoke to Abel his brother. And when they were in the field, Cain rose up against his brother Abel and killed him. Then the Lord said to Cain, "Where is Abel your brother?" He said, "I do not know; am I my brother's keeper?" And the Lord said, "What have you done? The voice of your brother's blood is crying to me from the ground. And now you are cursed from the ground, which has opened its mouth to receive your brother's blood from your hand. When you work the ground, it shall no longer yield to you its strength. You shall be a fugitive and a wanderer on the earth." Cain said to the Lord, "My punishment is greater than I can bear. Behold,

you have driven me today away from the
ground, and from your face I shall be hidden. I
shall be a fugitive and a wanderer on the earth,
and whoever finds me will kill me." Then the
Lord said to him, "Not so! If anyone kills Cain,
vengeance shall be taken on him sevenfold." And
the Lord put a mark on Cain, lest any who found
him should attack him. Then Cain went away
from the presence of the Lord and settled in the
land of Nod, east of Eden.

Once evicted from the Garden, Adam and Eve begin
their life outside of paradise. Soon, the very first pair of
brothers is born. With them comes the worst case of
sibling rivalry ever. Both of them compete for the approval
and affection of God. Only one seems to get it. In a pattern
that has become all too human, the jilted brother, Cain,
rises up and kills the one who found approval, Abel. The
curse of the Tree is in full force. Just out of the Garden,
and the sin of man has already degenerated into murder.

It is that sense of fear and inadequacy that overcomes
Cain. We do not live with the approval of the Father that
we possessed in the Garden, so we strive to find other
ways to feel important and accepted. This is what Cain
and Abel were seeking after in their sacrifice. They were
presenting gifts to God, to see if they were adequate. It
wasn't about the gift. It was about the person. It was
simply seeking approval from God.

For reasons that are not explained in the Bible, Abel's
sacrifice is accepted and Cain's is rejected. We know that it
is not the substance of the sacrifice that mattered. For
though Abel offered a sacrifice of flesh and Cain offered
one of wheat, God tells Cain that his sacrifice can be
acceptable. He tells him that "if you do well," then his
sacrifice would find approval with the Lord. By this we can
only assume that God's rejection had nothing to do with

the substance of the sacrifice. Cain's heart already harbored darkness, and the Lord could see it. For this reason, Cain was not accepted by God.

Jealousy grows in Cain. He sees his brother's sacrifice accepted while his is rejected. Compounding this jealousy is the fact that Cain blames Abel for his own rejection. He doesn't look into himself as the reason his sacrifice may have been rejected. Instead, following the pattern set out by his mother and father, he shifts the blame to another.

Cain reacts out of his fear and shame when he looks at Abel as the source of his problems. If he were to blame himself, then this would only increase his feelings of anxiety. If he were to admit that his sacrifice was rejected due to his own failings, then he would have to confront his sense of inadequacy. He would have to face his smallness and imperfection.

The Lord tells him this very thing. He tells Cain that it is his own fault and no other that his sacrifice has not been accepted. The advice that God gives Cain, "if you do well," indicates that he has not been doing well.

And Cain is clearly not doing well. Instead of confronting his sin, he allows it to dictate his feelings and thoughts. It is a pattern of behavior that should feel familiar to us all. We do not want to feel the vulnerability of facing our inadequate nature, our utter smallness, so we cover it up. We make excuses and pass blame.

We are also reminded in this passage that we are capable of confronting our sin and inadequacy. When God is speaking to Cain, reminding him that he must do well, he also warns him about the danger of letting sin fester in the heart. God warns that sin is couching at the door, and its desire is against you.

We are given the image of an enemy, hiding behind the door, unseen, ready to pounce, a wonderfully accurate image of sin. If it is at the door, then it has already invaded the house. The sin is within us. The sin lives inside of us. It is a danger we carry around with us all of the time. It is a danger that we should always be wary of, like an attacker waiting behind the door.

We are told that sin has a desire for us. But this desire is against us. The desire of sin is to destroy and consume. Once again, we see the enemy is within. Sin is not a friend. Sin wants to destroy us and undo us. To submit to the power of sin is to submit to our destruction.

But we should not fail to note that God tells Cain that he can overcome sin. He is capable of conquering the evil desires inside of him. God tells Cain directly that he "must rule over" his sin.

The word "must" that appears is the Hebrew word, timshel. It has been a bone of contention for translators for a while. No one can say for sure how to translate it correctly. Much has been made of this one word. One possible meaning for timshel is, "thou mayest", or, "you can." So it would not read, *you must* overcome sin, but, *you can* overcome sin. When God exhorts Cain, and warns him about sin, he is also reminding him that he is capable of overcoming the sin that seeks to destroy him. You can overcome it, God says. You may not, but you have the capability to decide to act differently.

If Cain falls prey to sin, it is because he chooses to. He chooses to allow sin dominion over his thoughts, his actions, and also his feelings. Sin does not control us against our will. It works within us as a conspirator against our life, but it does not command us.

Anytime we are faced with sin and temptation we have two distinct choices. The first is to admit that we have a failing, that we are sinners, and that we are being infected by an evil that lives in us and one that draws us away from God. The other option is to make excuses, to blame others, to blame God or fate, or convince ourselves it isn't that bad or it isn't wrong at all, or tell ourselves if it feels so right it couldn't be wrong. While the second option allows us to avoid our fears and inadequacies and presents us with an easier, more indulgent road, it is a lie. And because we believe that lie, we allow sin to overcome us. We tell ourselves that the enemy behind the door is no enemy at all. The real enemy are those outside, the ones that compound our fear and inadequacy.

So we lose the battle against sin on two different fronts. First, we allow the sin into us, that first evil thought, that first whisper of temptation. This may be a fact of human nature that we cannot prevent, being prey to temptation and evil. But we also lose in a second way, when we refuse to confront that sin. We pass the blame to others to protect our fragile pride. In refusing to confront that sin, we concede victory.

Cain submits to his sin. He does not resist it but indulges it. As the story unfolds, his heart darkens further. Cain leads his brother out into a field, rises up, and kills him.

But God hears Abel's blood. It cries out to him from the ground. Just as God sees every crime and injustice, he saw this one. Sin cries out to God, blood and murder cry out to God. There is no wrong that goes hidden from the heavens. Every act of disobedience and evil makes creation groan.

God confronts Cain about the awful sound of blood screaming from the earth. Cain does not answer, but dissembles. Am I my brother's keeper, he asks. Am I responsible for my brother? Why is his fate my business?

Of course, Cain is not his brother's keeper. Every adult human being is responsible for himself and where he is. But at the same time, Cain is responsible for his brother. For at that moment Abel lay in the ground, dead by his brother's hand. And Cain was responsible for that. He is not his brother's keeper, but he is responsible for what has happened to him.

None of us can say the same with a clear conscience either. Our actions, none of them, are free from the consequences that effect the people who share this planet with us. We can say in one respect, I am not my brother's keeper. We know we are not responsible for what our fellow man might do. Each person is as free as the other.

But we are also responsible for what happens to them. Nothing we do is without impact on others. The things we do, hardly, if ever, have a neutral impact on the world. All that we do affects our world and our society. Everything we do has an impact on other people. Our disregard, our lack of responsibility, even if it has no malice, can bring harm to others.

Later in Scripture, as God is giving the Law to his people, he tells them that if a man were to see his neighbor's cattle wandering into his field, he has an obligation to get that animal and bring it back to its rightful owner. In other words, he is commanded to look after the welfare of his neighbor, and even protect it.

You are not commanded to be your brother's keeper, for he is free and the keeper of his self. But you are commanded to be his neighbor. If you see one in injury or distress, to pass him by is to do him harm, for by your inaction you have allowed harm to overtake him. A thoughtless word can do unseen damage to the heart of another. Poison you dump in a river can be drunk by a child downstream. An unchecked fire can burn down an entire city. We do not have or bear responsibility for our neighbor's actions, but we must be responsible for how we affect one another. We must always consider the impact of what we say or do, or what we refuse to say and refuse to do.

We are not in charge of one another, but we are

responsible to one another. We may not be our brother's keeper, but we are his brother. And though we may not be responsible for his life, what we do or don't do can often be the difference between life and death.

Who of us, upon reading this story, does not feel at least a little sympathy towards the wayward Cain? We have all been in such a situation. It is one that we can readily identify with. We want to be accepted, we hunger for acceptance. We want it so badly it almost hurts—just a nod, a smile, any indication from the father that we are accepted and approved. The pain that follows when we do not receive that acceptance—who has not felt that heartache?

Of course, we cannot condone what Cain has done. It is not the fault of Abel that Cain was rejected. But we can understand the anger and humiliation that comes from such a rejection. It feels as if the whole world is lost to us, that we are alone. It makes us feel that we are fugitives and sojourners upon the earth with no place to call our own.

This is exactly the complaint that Cain makes to God when he is cast out and sent to the land of Nod. He has no place where he can belong. He is marked as rejected and unworthy. He is without protection and solace. The next person that sees him will surely take his life.

Though God cannot accept what Cain has done, or accept the sin that he bears in his heart, the Lord still shows him mercy. God can see into the heart, and though he sees the sin that Cain carries, he also sees the hurt. The Lord is angry with Cain, but has not yet given up on him. So he puts a mark on Cain. What it looks like, we do not know. But by this mark all who see it will know that Cain is under God's protection. It is a mark of mercy. Though Cain is a fugitive, perhaps he is not yet lost.

Some may feel that Cain has gotten off too easy, that Abel's murder has gone unpunished. Others might read this story and find it too harsh that God rejected Cain's sacrifice in the first place. Instead, what we should see is God displaying both his justice and his mercy.

It was justice that led God to reject Cain's sacrifice in the first place and bless Abel over his brother. It would not be just or fair to accept a sacrifice that is tainted with sin, and reward the one who gave it, as if it is as worthy as the other. That would be an injustice to Abel and to truth.

It was mercy that led God to allow Cain to live even after the murder he committed. He saw the hurt on Cain, knew the pain it caused him, but could not leave him completely unpunished. By his justice he cast him out of the land. He curses Cain that the land will no longer yield strength to him, cutting him off from a native power that existed in the early world. But by his mercy he makes it so that Cain has a chance to redeem himself. He doesn't give up completely on the wayward brother.

We will see these same aspects of God play out over and over again. Not only in the story of Genesis, but in the stories of our life, we will experience God's mercy and justice. By justice we are made to reap the consequences of our actions. By God's mercy we do not reap them fully, and we are given new opportunities to find redemption.

Justice demands that a price be paid for evil. There is no way to avoid this. But if justice was all we received, it would consume us completely, and even destroy us. Because God is merciful as well as just, he does not let this happen. We are made to feel the sting of his justice and also are allowed to experience the balm of his mercy. As the story of humanity unfolds, we will see God acting in justice and intervening in mercy, so that what he made and what he loves is not lost, but is brought closer to the fullness of its destiny.

6 - Genesis 6:1-7

The Corruption of the Earth

When man began to multiply on the face of the land and daughters were born to them, the sons of God saw that the daughters of man were attractive. And they took as their wives any they chose. Then the Lord said, "My Spirit shall not abide in man forever, for he is flesh: his days shall be 120 years." The Nephilim were on the earth in those days, and also afterward, when the sons of God came in to the daughters of man and they bore children to them. These were the mighty men who were of old, the men of renown.

The Lord saw that the wickedness of man was great in the earth, and that every intention of the thoughts of his heart was only evil continually. And the Lord regretted that he had made man on the earth, and it grieved him to his heart.

The story of Cain and Abel is the story of where Original Sin has taken us. The serpent, who originally corrupted Adam and Eve, through them has corrupted the entire human race. Murder rises up in the first siblings, and from there, evil is firmly established.

If we skip ahead in our story, past the lives of many generations, we see man multiplying as he was commanded, and spreading all over the earth. And with the multiplication of man has come the multiplication of sin. As human beings cover the earth, they cover it with evil.

Our story of the corruption of the earth picks up not with men, but with the angels. The Bible tells us in those days the sons of God fell in love, or developed a lust for human women. They took some of these women for wives. Or perhaps they took them as wives, meaning they gratified their lusts on them or ravished them.

Scripture does not say exactly who these creatures are. They are simply described as the "sons of God." Some have taken this to mean angels. Others have thought they might describe some other form of divine being or god in the divine council, part of the "us" described in 3:22. An old tradition calls these creatures the Watchers, special beings appointed to watch over mankind. They simply watched too closely. Some have even suggested the Bible is talking about extra-terrestrial creatures that flew down from space in those distant days to visit earth.

Whatever we may speculate, all that is clear from the story is that spiritual beings, something like angels or divine creatures, came from heaven down to earth to have sexual relations with women. What is also clear is that it is not right that they do this. For as soon as the Lord sees this happen, he sets a time limit on the life of man.

Before this, it was not unusual for man to live past 900 years. Now, a limit was set at 120. It seems like God did this as an early measure to stem the growth of evil. Put a limit on human years and you put a limit on the evil that he can commit. Or it may have been that the powers given to the creatures born of gods and men was too great, and some sort of limit must be put on their lives. For out of this union, between the sons of God and the sons of man, are born creatures that are called Nephilim.

Again, not much detail is given as to who these Nephilim are or what about them is so extraordinary. However, they are also referred to alongside giants and heroes of old, men of great power and renown. What appears to be described here is a mythic age. Many different cultures have legends of such a time in the

155

history of the world—an heroic age when humans with extraordinary abilities walked the earth. This was an age of epics, of creatures half-god and half-man. We can only speculate what they may have been capable of and what great feats they accomplished and what wonderful stories were spun off of their deeds. We have some hints in the world's mythologies, and if they are any indication, then it was an amazing age to live.

But it was also a horrible and dreadful time to be alive. The Bible does not go into detail about the accomplishments and stories of this mythic age because this story is not about heroes—this story is about corruption.

Mankind had grown corrupt. Evil had festered like a sore until it covered the whole earth. It is said that every intention and thought in man was "only evil" continually. Everything that man said and did was evil. Every thought and feeling in him was evil. The level of corruption was so great it is hard for us to imagine. As much as we would like to mourn about how evil and wicked our present generation has grown, we are nothing compared to the evil that proliferated in the days of Genesis six.

The corruption and wickedness of that day was so great that it spilled out over the earth and even infected the heavens. That is the point of the story about the sons of God being tempted by women and the birth of the Nephilim. It is to show us the level of corruption and evil in the world. What started in the heart of man now spread like a virus over all the earth until it infected the sons of God also. Now, they desired and lusted like human beings.

This is a strange idea to us. We don't think of earth as being able to affect the heavens, and certainly not corrupt them. Heaven to us is an inaccessible place to mortals, only entered into at death. Furthermore, heaven is a place that is beyond corruption, free from the taint of human evil and simple, earthly vice. It is the decrees of heaven that dictate what happens in the world beneath. Heaven is above, ruling and determining what happens on earth. Earth is below and follows and obeys what is determined from heaven.

But here we have something radically different. A unique sort of cosmology presents itself. This one describes an interplay between heaven and earth, an interchange of influence. We do not find a universe where heaven is the iron-fisted ruler of the earth, full of irrevocable fate and oracles of unavoidable doom. That is the heaven of astrologers and mediums, the readers of the stars and the witches of fate, the heavens of the Greek myths.

Instead, we see a heaven that is the abode of all spiritual, or heavenly creatures, good and evil alike. It is the heaven where even Satan appears, as in the beginning of the book of Job. Instead of being the exclusive domain of angels and good spirits, heaven is actually the place where all spiritual beings find their native place. Heaven is a realm, a spiritual realm, and while it may have its different levels, it is the abode of all spiritual creatures, good or evil. This is why at the end of Revelation, God creates a new heaven alongside the new earth. They both will be purged of evil.

We also see here a different relationship between heaven and earth. Not only does heaven influence the earth, but the earth is also able to influence heaven. Human, earthly corruption has insinuated itself into the heavenly realm. And human beauty has tempted the will of divine creatures.

The interplay described here is more fluid than we could ever have imagined. It is not just the heavens that influence earth, but the earth that can move the heavens. Or more accurately, human action and behavior can influence and move the heavens. For human beings are creatures of both earth and spirit. We are made of flesh, from the dust of the earth, as well as the breath of God, which gives us a divine spirit. So it makes sense, being partly spiritual creatures, that we might influence the environment of heaven.

What we have here is not only a unique cosmology, so different from the Greek outlook that portrays human beings as pawns to heaven and slaves to fate, but also a supreme human freedom. We are not bound by fate. For this reason the Jews were always forbidden to consult mediums or astrologers. It was a sin to consult the heavens as if fate were a thing written in stone. To do that would be to submit to spirits that man should not submit to. To consult fate or the stars would be to spurn the great gift, perhaps the greatest gift that God has given us—free will.

This is yet another reason why the argument between nature and nurture is a silly one. It is just another form of seeing man determined and bound by his fate. Instead of being bound by the decrees of heaven, those materialists would have us bound by the decrees of genes or environment. Like the ancient Greeks, they assume we are bound in some way, unable to decide or think or act under our own agency. True, there are influences all around us. There are temptations and desires that continue to pull at us. It is also true that we can give up our free will and be controlled by our temptations, be pulled by the influence of our culture, and allow ourselves to drift with the tide of fashion. But we do not have to do those things. We should not do those things. We were made to think, to decide, to consult our wisdom and the wisdom of God. We were made to be free creatures.

Unfortunately, man typically takes this gift of freedom and he binds it to the servitude of evil. He chooses what is wicked. Or rather, he lets wickedness be chosen for him. Mankind is free, but he inclines towards the bondage of evil. The serpent is indulged and runs free in our life. The serpent runs free until it touches every thought and feeling in man, until, like the people in this story, every thought and feeling in us is evil continually.

This is where our story has taken us, and for a moment leaves us there. Man has become so corrupt and evil his wickedness has spread to the heavens and brought low even the heavenly creatures. The situation has grown so dark and the earth so evil that God has regretted making mankind and has decided to wipe him off the face of the earth. For now, it seems like the serpent has won and he has taken over the earth. Mankind and life and the work of creation have failed.

God's great and risky gamble of making free will creatures has self-destructed and corrupted heaven and earth.

Part IV

-

The Dove

1 - Genesis 6:8-22

Noah

But Noah found favor in the eyes of the Lord.

These are the generations of Noah. Noah was a righteous man, blameless in his generation. Noah walked with God. And Noah had three sons, Shem, Ham, and Japheth.

Now the earth was corrupt in God's sight, and the earth was filled with violence. And God saw the earth, and behold, it was corrupt, for all flesh had corrupted their way on the earth. And God said to Noah, "I have determined to make an end of all flesh, for the earth is filled with violence through them. Behold, I will destroy them with the earth. Make yourself an ark of gopher wood. Make rooms in the ark, and cover it inside and out with pitch. This is how you are to make it: the length of the ark 300 cubits, its breadth 50 cubits, and its height 30 cubits. Make a roof for the ark, and finish it to a cubit above, and set the door of the ark in its side. Make it with lower, second, and third decks. For behold, I will bring a flood of waters upon the earth to destroy all flesh in which is the breath of life under heaven. Everything that is on the earth shall die. But I will establish my covenant with you, and you shall come into the ark, you, your sons, your wife, and your sons' wives with you. And of every living thing of all flesh, you shall bring two of every sort into the ark to keep them alive with you. They shall be male and female. Of the birds according to their kinds, and of the animals according to their kinds, of every creeping thing of the ground, according to its kind, two of every

*sort shall come in to you to keep them alive. Also
take with you every sort of food that is eaten, and
store it up. It shall serve as food for you and for
them." Noah did this; he did all that God
commanded him.*

The earth is full of evil and wickedness. The serpent
and all of his schemes, both the serpent within and the
serpent without, seem to have triumphed. The work of
creation is failing, free will has turned back on God, and
has followed after the desires of evil. All flesh has become
corrupt.

God looks down to the earth, and we are told he repents
or regrets ever making mankind. Human beings have
destroyed and made evil what God had created good. The
only way to save creation now is for God to intervene. But
corruption has become so dominant and pervasive, the
only way to save it is to start over again.

When we look at the flood, we tend to see it as an act of
God's great anger. It is an example unbelievers point to in
order to argue that the Christian God is a dark and
wrathful God. Look, they say, see how eager he was to
destroy the whole earth, see how angry and vengeful your
God is.

This part of the story is almost always misunderstood.
When God destroyed the world, it was not so much an act
of his anger, but of his salvation. God was not setting out
to punish the world as much as save it.

Scripture tells us God regretted ever making man. In
verse six it says that looking at what had become of
mankind and his world gave him grief. Grief, as anyone
knows who has gone through it, is a sense of profound
sadness when one experiences a loss. We grieve when we
lose something dear to us. It is a sensation of the heart
breaking over the loss of anything we love.

This was God's feeling at the outset of the flood story.

Anger is not his primary motive, but sadness. God looks down on his earth, he sees all that he is created, and he sees that it has become evil. The earth, we are told, was full of violence. Evil seeped into the very ground, it filled the air and polluted the water. All that God had made had fallen away into the clutch of evil. Why have we then, knowing what we know, assumed that this was an act of punishment? This was not an act of anger. It was an act of salvation. God was not trying to punish creation—he was in the act of saving it.

The forbearance and patience that God possesses was, is, and always will be, great. He tolerates the work and evil of man for a long time, grieving much, until he must act. In this case, he did not step in until only one man left in the entire world was righteous. He watched the earth grow worse and worse, and exercised patience as man turned away from him and followed after evil. He bore the wickedness of humanity until there was only one good person left on the earth.

It is always this way with God's anger. Even at Sodom and Gomorrah, even there he was willing to spare the city for a few righteous men. All it would take was a handful to forestall the wrath to come. And for the whole world he was willing to wait and give it chance after chance until it had gotten so bad only one option was left.

If God let it go even longer, waited even longer, then soon there would be no one righteous left at all. When Noah died or was killed by the violent world, there would be no good men in the world. Who would he be able to start over with if that were to happen? With no righteous men left, God would have no choice but destroy them all.

God was not giving up on his work of creation. Nor was he giving up on his work in humanity. He didn't decide that the whole work was a failure, destroy it all and start over again. Because he was preserving Noah, it was not a total do-over, but a restart. He kept a bit of the original material that he began with—the last of the seed of Adam—and went to work again. This was the only way to save his work. It was the first instance of reformation in the world. God was taking his work back to the beginning and starting over.

God is always saving. He is always working for good. He is always working to preserve and save those he has created. Even in the flood, God was a saving God.

But why must God kill all the animals too? Surely it was only man that had grown corrupt. It makes no sense that the animals must bear the guilt of mankind.

The animals did not bear guilt, but they did bear corruption. Like all of the earth, they had fallen and had been tainted with wickedness. It all stems from mankind and from man's wickedness. In his dominion over the earth, man has the capability to corrupt not only himself but also the creatures of the earth.

When God gave man dominion over the earth he gave him responsibility over the destiny of creation. With this came a power over the earth and the creatures that inhabit the earth. There is a connection and relationship between humanity and the earth. Just as in any relationship of leadership, as it goes with the leader it will go with those under the authority of a leader.

We see this in all forms of organizations. A toxic work environment is rightly blamed on toxic leadership, one which begins at the very top. To change the environment of any organization, one does best to change the leadership.

This is true for organizations of any size, from families all the way up to nations. An angry father will effect the whole mood and behavior of his family. A corrupt dictator will make for a corrupt nation. An evil king will cause the land suffer. A selfish CEO will bring ruin to his company.

The same concept holds true of the earth. Mankind has been appointed the keeper of the earth. As it goes with man it will go with the rest of creation. A corrupt and wicked mankind will produce a corrupt and wicked creation. It will be an earth of greater and more frequent disasters and disease. It will produce a planet that rebels, that breeds plague and famine, a planet that may even grow hotter and exhibit unpredictable and unstable weather patterns that threaten all life upon it.

In the same manner, a righteous humanity will produce a righteous planet. A good earth will proceed from a good humanity. It will be an earth that gives forth a grateful abundance. It will even be an earth of less disease and disaster, one without aberrant weather and famine.

To truly start over, all that man touched and influenced had to be destroyed. The population of the animals had to be reduced to where one man could influence and shape them again. With one righteous man left, it had to become a manageable load for him to oversee. Too many, and the wickedness of the old order may continue to spill over.

It grieved the heart of God when he looked at what he had made and saw that it had spoiled. What began as a beautiful garden of delight had degenerated into a world of violence and evil. God acted as only a loving God would. He acted to save his creation. He was saving his work. To do so he would have to destroy all that had become wicked and rebuild it again with what remained of goodness and light.

2 - Genesis 7:1-24

The Waters that Cleanse

In the six hundredth year of Noah's life, in the second month, on the seventeenth day of the month, on that day all the fountains of the great deep burst forth, and the windows of the heavens were opened. And rain fell upon the earth forty days and forty nights. On the very same day Noah and his sons, Shem and Ham and Japheth, and Noah's wife and the three wives of his sons with them entered the ark, they and every beast, according to its kind, and all the livestock according to their kinds, and every creeping thing that creeps on the earth, according to its kind, and every bird, according to its kind, every winged creature. They went into the ark with Noah, two and two of all flesh in which there was the breath of life. And those that entered, male and female of all flesh, went in as God had commanded him. And the Lord shut him in.

The flood continued forty days on the earth. The waters increased and bore up the ark, and it rose high above the earth. The waters prevailed and increased greatly on the earth, and the ark floated on the face of the waters. And the waters prevailed so mightily on the earth that all the high mountains under the whole heaven were covered. The waters prevailed above the mountains, covering them fifteen cubits deep. And all flesh died that moved on the earth, birds, livestock, beasts, all swarming creatures that swarm on the earth, and all mankind.

Everything on the dry land in whose nostrils was the breath of life died. He blotted out every living thing that was on the face of the ground, man and animals and creeping things and birds of the heavens. They were blotted out from the earth. Only Noah was left, and those who were with him in the ark. And the waters prevailed on the earth 150 days.

To save the earth God will cleanse it. It is not punishment or destruction he is after, but re-creation. He is going to start over, wash the stain from the earth put there by evil, and begin again with the only righteous man left and his family.

To accomplish this, God instructs Noah to build an ark. Within, he is to hold himself, his family, and a number of every animal to ride out the coming flood. When the waters recede, they are to go back out and return life to the planet.

Much has been debated about this incredible story. It has caused no end to wonder and incredulity. People have speculated and argued about the possibility that this really could occur. They have calculated how many animals could have really fit in an ark the size of the one described in Genesis. They ask if any evidence has ever been found of a worldwide deluge. Both sceptics and apologists have weighed in on the matter, both with good arguments.

The sceptics have pointed to the impossibility of the feat. And they produce very sane and convincing arguments. But, despite their insistence, they have not been able to kill faith in this story, nor rule out the possibility that it really did happen as described in the Bible.

Believers have made some good counter-arguments. Some have even reconstructed the ark to the exact specifications given to Noah. Others have pointed out that

169

a flood legend appears in almost every culture in the ancient world. But none of their arguments have been able to prove a worldwide deluge ever actually took place, or that a single family survived by building a boat and lasting out the flood.

I think an obsession on debating whether we can prove or disprove this event has robbed us of the greater understanding of the story. This story is about God's cleansing of the world. This is about his re-creation and God's commitment to his work.

By recreating instead of starting over, God is showing that his love remains for his original work. He does not just give up on what he has made, he does not give up on his world. If he has to, he will remake it. Reform, recreation, re-making—these are all the different ways of describing what God is doing in the world. If there is something wrong, something that must be changed, if it cannot be fixed, then God is ready to re-create.

God will keep the original form of what he did in order to preserve the thing he loves. This is true with the world in the day of Noah, as it is true with us in our daily lives. When there is wrong in us that cannot be corrected, God does not give up on his work. If needs be, he will re-create us, re-form us, re-make us, over and over again. It is a painful process, as we shall see in the work of the flood. But it is an option born out of genuine affection, for the only other option is total destruction and starting over.

As hard as the work of re-creation is, it is a sign of God's abundant love and of his unwavering commitment to us. He will not let us fester in the wrongness of our wicked ways. Even when we have gone wrong so deeply as to warp the essence of our being, he will re-create and re-form. He will keep what is essential. He will keep the heart of his creation, that heart which has been overwhelmed in the bogs of sin. He will clean it off, reshape it, and restore it to a right path. He is not a God who would give up on who we are meant to be until there is nothing left to restore, nothing left to be saved.

It is water God uses to cleanse the earth. The story says he opened the fountains of the deep and allowed the waters to rise until they cover the earth. This is not the first time we have encountered these waters of the deep. They were present at the very beginning. It was the waters of the deep that the spirit of God hovered over on the first day of creation. It was out of these same waters that God drew up the earth and made dry land. These are the waters from which creation originally sprang.

The heavens open up and rain falls on the earth. For forty days and nights the rain falls. It says the water piles on so deep that the highest mountain is covered up by fifteen cubits of water. That is approximately twenty-two feet over the highest mountain. When it is all done, the earth must have looked much as it had at the beginning. All the eye could see were the waters of the deep. One boat floats alone along its surface.

Since these waters were used at the outset of creation, it makes sense to use the same raw materials for re-creation. Aside from this, water is the perfect cleaner. It is a universal solvent, so even the iniquity of man is dissolved in its depths and washed away. This is why we always clean with water. It seems to make everything new again, even the human body.

As the earth gets covered in water, it returns to the womb. Now, it can be remade. Like all rebirths, it must first have a death. So the earth dies and returns to a primordial state. Only now can it have a chance to start over.

It was much like a baptism for the earth. It was submerged in the water, experiencing a death. Within, its sins and stains were washed away. The wicked earth, just like the old, wicked self, was drowned by grace. This death was, of course, painful, but absolutely necessary. It submerged only to reemerge. It died to live again. It was covered in waters, not to be punished, but to be remade.

3 - Genesis 8:1-19

The Dove

But God remembered Noah and all the beasts and all the livestock that were with him in the ark. And God made a wind blow over the earth, and the waters subsided. The fountains of the deep and the windows of the heavens were closed, the rain from the heavens was restrained, and the waters receded from the earth continually. At the end of 150 days the waters had abated, and in the seventh month, on the seventeenth day of the month, the ark came to rest on the mountains of Ararat. And the waters continued to abate until the tenth month; in the tenth month, on the first day of the month, the tops of the mountains were seen.

At the end of forty days Noah opened the window of the ark that he had made and sent forth a raven. It went to and fro until the waters were dried up from the earth. Then he sent forth a dove from him, to see if the waters had subsided from the face of the ground. But the dove found no place to set her foot, and she returned to him to the ark, for the waters were still on the face of the whole earth. So he put out his hand and took her and brought her into the ark with him. He waited another seven days, and again he sent forth the dove out of the ark. And the dove came back to him in the evening, and behold, in her mouth was a freshly plucked olive leaf. So Noah knew that the waters had subsided from the earth. Then he waited another seven days and sent forth the dove, and she did not return to him anymore. In the six hundred and first year, in the first month, the first day of the month, the waters were dried from off the earth. And Noah removed the covering of the ark and looked, and behold, the face of the ground was dry. In the second month, on the twenty-seventh day of the month, the earth had dried out. Then God said to Noah, "Go out from the ark, you and your wife, and your sons and your sons' wives with you. Bring out with you every living thing that is with you of all flesh—birds and animals and every creeping thing that creeps on the earth—that they may swarm on the earth, and be fruitful and multiply on the earth." So Noah went out, and his sons and his wife and his sons' wives with him. Every beast, every creeping thing, and every bird, everything that moves on the earth, went out by families from the ark.

The world has been flooded in an act of God's salvation. Noah and all the animals are tossed on the waters, their world destroyed. But God has not forgotten Noah and the role he will play in the new world. He commands the deep to close its doors and he shuts the windows of heaven. The rain stops and the waters rise no more.

Stuck in the ark as he is, Noah has no way of knowing if the world is safe, or when he will be able to emerge from his confinement. We are told God had shut Noah up in the ark, so there are no decks to walk outside of the ship or windows that would afford him a view of the land. There is no way, in other words, for Noah to determine when it would be safe to emerge again into the world.

At this point in the story we are introduced to another animal. The first animal that was mentioned by name was the serpent. We found him to be a spirit of cleverness and intelligence, but also one of pride and willfulness. It is a creature that lodges within us and can cause no end of misery.

The next creature that is named in the Bible is the raven. Because he cannot see what the world is like outside the ark, Noah sends a raven out to be his eyes in the world. We are told this bird flies around until the waters dry up, but never returns to Noah. Whatever it was about the raven, he proved inadequate.

The next animal we come to is much more helpful - the dove. After the raven fails to return, it is this bird that Noah uses next. It is with the dove that Noah finds his true help.

Birds were always considered special animals. They possess that unique quality of being creatures of heaven and earth. They hop along the ground on feet like the rest of terrestrial creatures, but they can also spread out their wings and dwell as denizens of heaven. They touch the realm of God and the angels as well as the abode of animals. For thousands of years they have been regarded as divine messengers. They are the source of oracles and signs. They soar up in the sky and talk to the citizens of heaven. Then they touch the earth and speak with humans as well.

Among birds, the dove finds a special place in Christian folklore. The dove has long been a symbol of purity and holiness, and God's presence and communication with his people. It is often a representative of the Holy Spirit, the vehicle which God uses to act and communicate with his people. After all, it was in the form, or likeness, of a dove that the Holy Spirit came down and dwelt upon Jesus when he was rising out of the waters after his baptism.

What we learn here is that we have a power of discernment within us other than the serpent. We also have a dove. We do not just have that part of us that is intelligent and clever, and being prideful insists on relying on its own intelligence. There is also a capacity in us for something good and right and holy, and is eager to trust in the will of God. We have the serpent within. But we also have the dove.

The dove is that special, innate capacity we possess that allows us to not always trust in ourselves, but to trust in God. We are more than rational creatures who fester with an insistent will that things be done our own way. We are more than animals of selfish pride. We are creatures that can reach out to the will of God and put aside our desires and follow the will of the Father. The dove is that aspect we carry within us.

For certain, there is evil in us. There is the serpent who tempts us with evil desires and to the path of our own wisdom. But there are good impulses in us as well. There is a part of us that wants to obey God, that wants to do good. There is the drive in us to do what is acceptable to our heavenly Father and receive his approval. There is a desire in us to do what is right. We all have a serpent, and we all have a dove.

To rely on, and live in, our serpent selves is to lean upon our own understanding. It is to do what we want and act in a way that looks good in our own eyes. It is that part of us that believes we can determine what is right and wrong on our own. It considers what is good for us, and makes no regard for the impact it will have on others or the plan of God. It is the path that leads us by pride and sin.

To rely upon the dove, to consult and act with the dove, is to rest on the wisdom and will of God. Noah did not try to figure out for himself if it was safe to leave the ark. Instead, he consulted the dove. He did not lean on or trust his own understanding, he consulted the wisdom of God.

This is not to say that we are never to use our own

intelligence. Through the majority of the day, and majority of our life, we must rely upon our intellect and our wisdom to make decisions and try to figure out what is right. If Noah had a window in the boat through which he could see the world or a deck to walk upon, he could have done the same. But he had none of these things. He had nothing which his own intelligence could assess. So he had to rely upon the instruction and word of God.

Even our intelligence is useless to us unless it is taught in the right way. The serpent within can do nothing but deceive us unless it is taught how to think and reason, and more importantly, submit to the wisdom of God. Without the foundation of truth, spoken to us by and through the word of God, our capacity for reasoning will be faulty at best. Without God's word, manifest and spoken in us by the dove, our reasoning and thinking, the very highest achievements of our intellect, will be but selfish musings and justifications to pursue what we desire. It will be darkened and led astray. Truth will run from us and slip from our fingers. Understanding will not make its home in our minds. We will be perpetually certain of ourselves, while in reality perpetually confused. Without the dove, the serpent will know nothing that is true. Without God's spirit, to manifest and reveal what is true and right, our minds have no foundation upon which we can build a mind of wisdom. In all things, we must submit to God's ways and God's wisdom.

There are many times when we face something beyond our intelligence. Either we cannot grasp what is happening, we cannot understand what is going on, or it is something that cannot be comprehended by the human mind. No matter how much we believe in the power of the intellect to be able to grasp all things, there are some simply beyond our reasoning power. Some things are inaccessible to our wisdom. Some things we will never know and never understand.

We are not without guidance in these times. It was for such times that the dove was given to us. We all possess that power and capacity in us. We can access the guidance and the instruction of God. We can reach out in faithful prayers in moments of distress, hardship or confusion, and send our dove out to seek the will of God.

It was not in his intelligence and assessment that Noah relied and trusted. He sent out, and relied upon the dove. He was seeking instruction from the wisdom of God.

Note how the dove responded to Noah when he set her out upon the waters. She did not return Noah a direct and explicit message from God. She did not say, "Stay in the boat," or "The waters remain," or "All is safe." Instead, when Noah set the dove out of the ark, she responded in three different ways. One time the dove returned. The second time she returned with an olive branch. The third time she did not return at all.

These are the different types and ways that God will often respond to us when we seek him out. Sometimes, our words simply return to us. There is no meaningful response, or rather nothing we feel is communicated. This usually means we must wait. Stay the course, do as you are, remain on the road you travel now.

Sometimes God gives us a clear sign. When the dove returned with the olive branch she was communicating something specific to Noah. The waters are quickly subsiding, the time is near. Many times, God speaks to us in various signs: a word from another believer, a coincidence that cannot be ignored, the fortunate (or unfortunate) convergence of events that makes his will quite clear. Signs like these are more abundant than we believe or notice, and we would do well to pay them heed.

The third time the dove didn't return. This time, the sign, or communication, was obvious. The waters had receded. These are the most direct forms of a word we get from the Lord. This is not a sign or a door closed, but a door thrown wide open. This is like those rare times when God paves a way for us so that his will is not in any doubt. We crave and cherish these times, though they are rare.

This is, of course, not an exact or comprehensive way in which God communicates his will to us or how we can access the divine. These are merely examples inspired by the story of Noah and how the dove spoke with him. What is important to remember is that we have an instinct and desire for good as well as for evil. We have direction and guidance from our created natures as well as our fallen natures. Too often, we allow the serpent free reign in our life. His advice is always the easiest advice to follow. To obey the dove is almost always more work.

But we are not left alone in the world, left to battle the serpent who seeks to undo us, and undo all of life. God has given us the dove as well, a capacity to lean on his wisdom, be taught by his word and revelation, and even access the divine will by the action of the spirit. It often will not speak as we would desire, but he does speak to us, and he does offer us guidance and wisdom when we need it the most. More specifically, he offers us guidance and wisdom when we seek it from him.

The dove is that divine impulse to work with the will of God. It desires to see all that God desires. It works to fulfill all that God would fulfill in us and the world. As the serpent is the will and work of the self, it works against the will of God, for it would see the self glorified above all. But the dove desires the glory of God, and if it desires any glory for itself, it is only the glory that God would bestow upon us, the only glory that we could truly possess because it is given by our Creator and God.

Good things happen when we trust in God's wisdom over our own, when we allow truth to teach us. We gain a foundation of wisdom in which our own mind and intelligence grows wise, more so than it ever could on its own. We can see more clearly who we are and see the world as it is. We can access a wisdom far beyond our own when we allow the dove to dwell in us.

Life happens when we trust in the dove. Life increases in us and it increases in the world. The work of God is advanced, and we find a peace and confidence when we are in the will and work of God.

When the flood dries up and God releases Noah and his family from the ark, as they step out into the world that still glistens with the cleansing waters, he gives them a command. Be fruitful and multiply, God tells them. It is the same command that he gave to humanity when he first made them. What was determined for man at his creation, is commanded again when he is redeemed. The original purpose and intent of creation continues. The work of God is not only starting over, but it also remains the same. Mankind is being sent out into the world again. The last time, he was driven out, chased from Eden and expelled from paradise. This time, he is being redeemed, released from the confinement of the ark and welcomed into the new world. Last time, he was driven from his home, the serpent biting at his heels. This time, he is led out into a recreated earth, following the promise of the dove.

4 - Genesis 8:20-22

The Covenant

Then Noah built an altar to the Lord and took some of every clean animal and some of every clean bird and offered burnt offerings on the altar. And when the Lord smelled the pleasing aroma, the Lord said in his heart, "I will never again curse the ground because of man, for the intention of man's heart is evil from his youth. Neither will I ever again strike down every living creature as I have done. While the earth remains, seedtime and harvest, cold and heat, summer and winter, day and night, shall not cease."

The flood has ended and Noah comes down the mountain with his family and all the animals inside, emerging from the ark after a long confinement. He and his family have survived the destruction of the world. No other human being, past or present, can boast of such a feat.

The first thing Noah does as he emerges from the ark is build an altar to the Lord. He then takes one of every clean animal and one of every clean bird and makes a sacrifice to God. The aroma of this burnt offering floats up to heaven. God smells the aroma of Noah's offering, and we are told the smell was pleasing to the Lord.

This passage might seem strange to the modern sensibility. We, who have been thousands of years removed from animal sacrifice to God, may not understand the significance of this, or why this pleases God. We have come to understand God as spirit, and not one who consumes food as we do, or would be enticed by the smell of it.

But, we are told that the aroma of this sacrifice was, in fact, pleasing to God. I would think it was not the actual smell as we understand it that God approved of, but the sentiment behind the sacrifice. When Noah was sacrificing, he was showing thanksgiving to God. After all of his trials, over 200 days shut up in the ark while a storm raged outside, and then to emerge and find that he and his family were all that was left of humanity—after all this, Noah survived. As he stepped out onto the slope of Mount Ararat, the first solid ground his feet had touched in a long time, his first thought was to thank the God who delivered him.

This is what made the aroma pleasing to God. It was not the smell of cooking meat that God enjoyed, rather it was the thanksgiving and gratitude behind it. Like in the offering of Cain and Abel, it was not the physical substance of sacrifice that made Abel's acceptable to God, it was the sentiment behind the sacrifice that God finds pleasing.

There is very little that we can actually give God. The whole earth belongs to him. The universe, in fact, is his. What does man have that we can ever offer to God?

There are only four things that a human being can ever give God. We can give him honor. We can give him obedience. We can give him love. And we can give him our gratitude. Honor, obedience, love and gratitude—these are the gifts of man to our God. And this is all he asks of us.

Through all of Noah's trials, he gave to God these gifts, all that we can truly give him. His righteousness in a world of evil was both honor and love to God. By building the ark, he was showing obedience. Finally, as he emerged from the ark, he gave God his gratitude. Out of this gratitude came a sacrifice. And as the aroma of that gratitude climbed unto the heavens, it pleased God.

God found this aroma of gratitude so pleasing that he made a promise. It was directed towards Noah, but it concerns every one of us. God promised never to wipe all of life from the earth again. The flood would be the first and last time this would happen. Every time after this, even unto this very day, when God tolerates the evil that man does, this is partly why. When someone asks why God allows so much wickedness on the earth, we can say it is because he made a promise to Noah, never to destroy all life from the earth again.

This is the amazing nature of God's blessing. When God gives his blessing, it is not just the object of that blessing that prospers (the one who is blessed), but the people around and related to that person who receive the benefits of that blessing. Children are blessed because of the piety of their parents. Nations are blessed because of the righteousness of their leaders. Communities that do not know God are blessed because of groups that exist within them that seek out the will of God.

God's blessing is one that overflows. Like it says in the Psalm, "my cup runneth over." The blessing of our Lord is one that is lavished with excess. Many, who were not the original objects, are blessed by it. Much of the favor we receive from God today could be the result of something one of our ancestors did. In the same way, our obedience and gratitude could result in blessings for generations after we are gone, just as we are still being blessed today by the aroma of sacrifice that Noah offered God those many years ago. It was from that sacrifice that God promised never to destroy the earth again because of man's wickedness.

There was another reason why God made this promise. It was not just because of Noah's gratitude. God also promises not to destroy the earth again because man's heart will always be inclined towards evil. He says that from his youth, the intention of man's heart is evil. The flood, God acknowledges, does not wipe evil from the earth, only that present incarnation of evil. It gave creation a chance to start over, but it does not solve the problem of evil. And since the problem of evil will always be on earth as long as men walk the earth, God will not destroy, or punish the earth again because of man's wickedness.

Evil is not just something mankind does now and again. It is not an anomaly to be wondered at. What God acknowledges here is that evil is a part of man's nature. He will be wicked from youth. His thoughts will be consumed with what is evil. This is what mankind will have to contend with for as long as mankind walks the earth.

The theological term for this is "total depravity." It means that the nature of man, all the way to the core of his being, has been warped and distorted by sin. Everything we do, even the good things, have been touched with sin. The serpent has coiled itself around the heart of man, and we must contend with it in everything we do.

This is a difficult thing for us to admit. It is not just that man's intentions are touched with evil, but his nature is. God is talking about us here. Our thoughts—yours and mine—are evil from our youth. Evil is a part of our nature.

The danger that all humanity fell into is our danger. The promise that God made to Cain, that he can overcome or master the temptation in him is a promise that is ours as well. This is something we must all face about our nature if we are to be honest about ourselves and care anything about truth. The serpent is us.

The dove is also us, an impulse for good, but we are usually disinclined to obey the dove. Evil appeals much more to our free natures. When we do what is evil, we believe we are doing what we want. We feel we are following our own desires when we submit to sin. Temptation looks fun and pleasurable and is filled with so many immediate rewards. It proves irresistible because it comes from our core, and it indulges our pride, vanity and desire for self-mastery.

Evil is easy, even instinctive for us.

Good, on the other hand, is difficult. Doing what is right always takes work. Wisdom and study are required to know truth. Endurance and strength are required to resist temptation. To do good means to put aside our own wants and look after the needs of another. To do good requires us to stay awake all night to guard over the weak, or travel a great distance to help another, or give away what we own, or forego our rights, or swallow an insult, or forgive a wrong. To do good requires us to resist the more powerful of the two impulses inside us. Good is often not fun, or pleasurable, or satisfying to our self-interest. It even feels like it goes against our nature.

To be honest, it does go against our stronger nature. In the human animal, the serpent feels more natural than the dove—indulgence more natural than denial. It is not that self-interest is always bad, but when evil does rise up in us, it almost always does so in the name of self-interest. The struggle against evil is a difficult struggle. Alone, it would be impossible to resist. But just as there is an enemy within, there is also a friend given to us by our Creator. The dove can guide us. The dove will guide us. But we must open ourselves to its guidance. We must put aside ourselves and allow God to act in us. We must follow not our nature but God's call and the dove's impulse in us. As we feed the dove and ignore the serpent, what is good grows strong in us, and what is evil withers and starves. It never totally disappears, but it can grow weaker. The serpent will always be a part of our nature, always a force that we must contend with. It is when we believe there is no evil in us, or that we have overcome the evil in our life, that we are most vulnerable to the serpent rising again in power over us. We must always be aware of the wickedness that nurses in our own heart. By the grace of God we may overcome. By his goodness and spirit, which dwell in us like a dove, we may do what is good. We can resist temptation. We can do what is right. We can crush the power of the serpent within us and allow the dove to reign. By the grace of our Maker and our God, the one who became our Redeemer, we can.

In the midst of the struggle, as we do what is good, as we give God our honor, our obedience, our love, and our gratitude, it rises like a pleasing aroma to heaven. Out of this comes blessing. Not just for ourselves, but the whole earth. When God blesses us, it is a blessing that touches generations that follow after us. Hundreds of years from now, when people are enjoying the blessing of God, it could be because of our obedience today that they enjoy it. It was because of Noah's obedience and Noah's gratitude that the whole world received a blessing. Even until this very day, that blessing continues. It was because of Noah that still today the promise of God continues that, "While the earth remains, seedtime and harvest, cold and heat, winter and summer, day and night, shall not cease."

5 - Genesis 9:1-7

Blessings, Warnings and a Sign

And God blessed Noah and his sons and said to them, "Be fruitful and multiply and fill the earth. The fear of you and the dread of you shall be upon every beast of the earth and upon every bird of the heavens, upon everything that creeps on the ground and all the fish of the sea. Into your hand they are delivered. Every moving thing that lives shall be food for you. And as I gave you the green plants, I give you everything. But you shall not eat flesh with its life, that is, its blood. And for your lifeblood I will require a reckoning: from every beast I will require it and from man. From his fellow man I will require a reckoning for the life of man.

"Whoever sheds the blood of man,
*   by man shall his blood be shed,*
* for God made man in his own image.*
*   And you, be fruitful and multiply, increase greatly on the earth and multiply in it."*

Though the recreation of the earth is complete, things will not go back to the way they were. Sin has irrevocably altered the earth. Life on this planet will truly never be the same. It may have been redeemed from its sin, but paradise is still lost. The separation from our blissful state in the garden only increases.

It says that the fear of man will be upon the animals of the earth. Never again will it be like it was in Eden, when the animals walked tamely up to the man for him to grant them names. Even leading up to the flood, we can assume that the animals were tame, or at least they did not flee from man. Or there was at least enough peace between the animals and man that Noah was able to gather them all in the ark.

Now, this will no longer be the case. We take another step away from paradise. The peace that existed among the creatures of the earth is broken. The animals that once were tame and obeyed us will turn and run from us in fear, and some will even attack us.

It seems the fear is for good reason. For God also in this passage has given the animals for man to eat. Before, people lived as vegetarians. In the Garden, he ate freely and in ease from the trees. After, when he had to work the earth, man ate from the produce of farming. Now, for the first time, he will eat the flesh of animals.

The disturbance of earthly harmony continues. The animals will flee from us. We will pursue the animals for food. Any and all vestiges of paradise continue to crumble away. Man's dominion is fading, or rather turning into a ghost of itself. Sin and evil, introduced into the earth by man, are eating away at the purity and goodness of creation. Even the order of creation is deteriorating.

Our banishment from the Garden is complete. All the remnants of paradise have been removed. Our lives have been shortened. Our food source has gone from easy vegetarian to flesh eating hunter. Our dominion and peace with the rest of the animals has turned to fear. The earth has moved on from paradise. Man has become something almost unnatural. Iniquity, evil, and sin have changed the world forever.

As a sign of how awful this state of affairs has become, human beings are given their first law. This is not a good thing. This is not a sign that we are headed in a right direction. Laws are only given when something wrong is being committed. And an abundance of laws indicates an abundance of evil and wrongdoing. We bring in laws, and begin to establish them, when our lawlessness and evil must be restrained.

The command that God gives us is a command against the shedding of human blood. Later, this command shall reappear as, "Thou shall not murder." But they are the same—we shall not shed the blood of our fellow man. Because each one of us is made in the image of God, life is sacred. None of us should commit that most awful of sins and rob from another human being that which was given by God. It is not only a sin against a fellow man but also a sin against the God whose image dwells in each and every person.

This is a dimension of sin that we hardly think about or entertain, that we could sin against the image of God. When we commit wrongs against our neighbor, especially wrongs that bring shame and dishonor to him, we are sinning against the image of God in him. When we commit shameless acts in our own bodies, we are not perpetuating a victimless crime, for we are also sinning against the image of God within us. All sin bears this awful weight, that it threatens more than the body or the mind, but the sacred image of the divine in which we are formed.

Instead, we ought to bring honor to the image of God, the image within us and the image that is borne upon the soul of our fellow humans. The first and most important way we do this is in preserving human life. Human life is most sacred for this reason, and for this reason it should be guarded above other forms of life.

Because God needed to make this command against murder, it may give us an insight into the antediluvian world. Since God had a need to forbid murder, it is likely that murder was widespread in the pre-flood world. This is the wickedness and evil that so offended and outraged God. Murder was creeping in and proliferating all over the

189

earth, man taking the life of man, and so making the earth cry out with all the blood spilled upon it.

So God makes it clear that we understand how wicked it is to take the life of another human being. Human life is sacred. Human life should not be taken. This is the first law of God and by this we can understand that it is the most sacred law we possess. No society can be good that allows murder, and no society can be blessed where murder occurs unpunished. It may even be an accurate measure of the goodness of a culture by how they respect and honor life. A culture that honors life—all life—is a good culture. One that shows disrespect for God's work by allowing murder, whether it is the killing of the very old by neglect, or the not-yet born by medical procedure, shows a contempt for God's creation and violates this first and essential command given to us by God.

There is a penalty laid upon anyone who would violate this command. This stresses the seriousness of the order. There will be consequences, the Lord tells us. For if any person sheds the blood of another, his blood will be required of him. If you kill, then you shall be killed. And it is not God who will do this. Man himself will be required to see that the punishment is duly executed, for he says that as man sheds the blood of another, by man his blood shall be shed.

What God requires here is called atonement. For this evil act of murder there will be a reckoning that is required, a balancing of accounts. A price must be paid for an evil done. For blood that is shed, blood will be required.

To demand this is not a curse. God does not require the life of a murderer simply to punish one who has committed the act. This is the work of redemption. For every murder, every drop of human blood spilled, the earth cries out for justice. The world is thrown out of balance. A reckoning is required to put the earth right again. The accounts must be settled. An injustice done to one requires that same act be committed upon the perpetrator, thus bringing the world to balance again, so the infection of evil can be kept at bay.

What a sad state of affairs that man has made of the world. This is all the consequence of human evil. Any failure of the earth can be traced back to us as keepers of the earth. Wielding a greater influence than we possibly realize, our evil causes the world to fail. In direct and indirect ways, we distort and destroy creation, putting all of it out of balance and bringing disaster to everyone and everything that lives on the planet.

Because of our evil, all manner of curses have fallen on man and beast alike. Because of our evil, nature that was made to glorify its Creator has fallen and shattered into plague and earthquake and fire. Because of our evil, the very nature of the wild has changed, dangerous and deadly, a nature red in tooth and claw.

Pollution doesn't harm the earth near as much as human sin. Pollution itself is an outcome of sin, yet another form of evil. No one can deliberately and knowingly poison the earth and air, destroy the beauty and vitality of the planet, while saying he is being obedient to God.

Amid this despairing state of affairs, the Lord gives us hope. He makes a covenant with Noah. Actually, he makes a covenant with Noah, with all creatures with him in the ark, and with the earth. Never again will the Lord wipe out all life with the waters of the flood. It is a one-sided covenant, for he asks nothing of man here. Instead, he makes a promise to all creation. He will never again destroy all life with a flood.

He gives himself a sign of this promise, something to remind himself of what he said. It is the bow in the clouds, what we call a rainbow. It spreads across the sky only after a rain. It is there to remind God of the promise that he made, to not allow the rains and waters to wipe out all life again.

Surely it is meant as a comfort to us as well. For as we fear the waters rising, and we fear their destructive power, we can have faith that life will go on. God will not destroy the world with flood. From here on out, his plan of redemption will be different. That plan begins with a covenant.

God will still work to redeem the earth. As long as there is evil in the world and evil in the heart of man, God will work to redeem us from our own sin and our own tendencies towards self-destruction. But he will not do it through a flood. And it appears that he will not do it again through world-wide destruction. From here on, he will redeem through the work of covenant.

We that have read ahead and know the rest of the story—we know the covenant that is made, as we know why that covenant failed. It failed because of man's sinfulness. When that happens, God redeems through blood. But that is another story. Rather, that is the story of humankind.

But for now, God has redeemed the earth. He has saved it from the wickedness that threatened to drown his creation in blood. God puts the bow in the sky to remember never to destroy the world again in water. The sign is for him to remember his promise.

It is interesting that it should be for God and not for us. Why would God need a reminder? Perhaps it is because he knows man will continue to tempt his anger with his love of all things wicked. Maybe God chooses to have a reminder because he knows he will continue to be antagonized by man to wrath. He knows, as he said, that man is wicked from birth. Despite the love of God, and despite all he has given us, man will still incline his heart to evil, embracing what is wrong and rejecting what is good.

The sign, we are told, the rainbow in the sky, is for God to remember. But we should look and remember too. Every time we see the rainbow we should remember what God has promised. We can look and know that the earth will abide, not by our goodness, but by the continued mercy of God. It is a mercy to which he has committed himself. In fact, he is so committed to it that he gave himself a reminder.

6 - Genesis 11:1-9

The Tower of Babel

Now the whole earth had one language and the same words. And as people migrated from the east, they found a plain in the land of Shinar and settled there. And they said to one another, "Come, let us make bricks, and burn them thoroughly." And they had brick for stone, and bitumen for mortar. Then they said, "Come, let us build ourselves a city and a tower with its top in the heavens, and let us make a name for ourselves, lest we be dispersed over the face of the whole earth." And the Lord came down to see the city and the tower, which the children of man had built. And the Lord said, "Behold, they are one people, and they have all one language, and this is only the beginning of what they will do. And nothing that they propose to do will now be impossible for them. Come, let us go down and there confuse their language, so that they may not understand one another's speech." So the Lord dispersed them from there over the face of all the earth, and they left off building the city. Therefore its name was called Babel, because there the Lord confused the language of all the earth. And from there the Lord dispersed them over the face of all the earth.

After the flood, humanity begins to spread and multiply as they were commanded. They migrate from the east to a place called Shinar. There, they begin to build a tower, one that is so big its top reaches the very heavens. The building of this tower offends God. He doesn't like the fact that it is being built and he seems to like even less the potential that mankind exhibits in undertaking, and succeeding, in such a project. So he gathers the "us" that have been mentioned before, and they confuse the languages of man, making cooperation impossible. Before, it seems there was only one language that people spoke. Then, God stirs them up so that their tongues are confused and they begin to speak different languages. The different languages separate the people, and unable to understand one another, they wander away from the city and leave the tower unfinished.

At first glance we cannot tell why God is so angry. The Bible doesn't tell us that the tower is being built for an evil purpose, like to serve a false god. It says that it is simply a tower that reaches to the heavens. What God notices, and what he says to the mystery beings that surround him, is that nothing will be impossible for man if he is united like he is at that moment. Nothing that he sets out to do will be denied him. So God confuses their languages and scatters the people.

There must be more to the story than a first, surface reading would suggest. This is more than God simply feeling jealous of man or inconvenienced by the people building towers. There was something about the city, or the tower itself, that offended God. There was some reason man's unity had to be disturbed.

The tower is the focus of the story, and therefore our clue as to why God had to scatter the people. It is said that their intent was to build a tower with its top in the heavens. This can mean one of two things. Either 1) it was going to be a tower that was really tall. The heavens were what they called the sky, and being so tall it would touch the sky. Or 2), it was a tower that in some way would challenge heaven and the authority of God.

I remember as a child, through my own imagination and reading some fictional works regarding the tower, believing something dark and sinister was at hand. I thought of the people of Shinar building the tower in order to reach heaven itself. Upon reaching heaven, they would bore through the walls and invade. Since God couldn't have men getting into heaven, he confused their languages and destroyed the tower.

We cannot know for sure what the intention or purpose of the tower was. Nor can we say for sure why it was offensive to God. Perhaps, there was some clear, evil purpose in its building. Perhaps, it did serve a pagan god. But in reading this story, and considering just what we are told, it seems clear that the reason they built the tower was to make a monument to themselves.

What they said was, "in order to make a name for ourselves," and so we will not be "dispersed over the earth." When the people of Shinar were building the tower, they did so to make a monument to themselves. They sought to bring glory to their name and their culture. They desired that their renown would never be forgotten. They were to build it and say, "Look how great we are. Let generations gaze upon what we have done and marvel at us."

It was this pride that was offensive to God. It was this drive for self-glorification that caused the Lord to look down upon the building of the tower with disapproval. For though man had, and would, continue to build monuments to himself, this was to be the greatest, for it would reach the very heavens.

This was a common practice in the ancient world, so the impulse did not desert people after they were scattered. Ancient cultures are covered with great monuments, from towers to pyramids, obelisks, gardens and even cities. Pharaohs, kings and emperors were obsessed with the idea of building structures that would live past them. They wanted to be sure that their name lived on after their death. They wanted to be certain that their glory would be known to future generations.

If this idea seems foreign, just remember that our culture preaches something very similar. It may not be in monuments of stone, but we still encourage the glorification of the self. They call it self-promotion, or getting the most out of life, but the deeper message is the same. We are told that we must make our mark upon the world, stand out from the crowd, make people take notice and remember that we were there.

Leaders today are obsessed about their legacy. They want to be remembered for their treaties or programs. We name bridges and roads after them, as well as schools and legislation. They fight over who is responsible for the success of a successful economy and who is at fault for dragging the nation down into poverty.

Nor is the common man free from this drive to glorify the self. We want to make sure we get credit for what we have done. We want to be remembered and noticed. We strive to stand out from the crowd and be recognized as unique. We want people to be envious of our life, so much so that we are careful to present only a meticulously crafted picture of that life, featuring only our triumphs and joys. We are a people who walk around with cameras in our pockets, yet the most frequent picture we take is of our self.

We work very hard to glorify the self, even if that means presenting an illusion to the world. Even though we know it is an illusion, we will prefer this illusion for reality because this illusion will give us the one thing we are truly after—for others to look at us and give us glory.

We still yearn for what we have lost in the Garden. God walked with us in the cool of the evening. We were confident in our self, because we knew that God loved and treasured us. Instead, all we can see today is our nakedness. We can only see how inadequate we are. In that hunger, we seek to fill it in the way that we see best— to lift up and glorify the self. That is what the work of our life has become, to glorify the self, to make a name for the self, to make people sit up and take notice of us and declare how wonderful we are.

This will never fulfill us, and it will always fail because man was not made to glorify himself. Man's proper work is to glorify God. Our lives will never be fulfilled in seeking to make ourselves great, in magnifying our own name. We will not find what we are looking for in building towers for ourselves.

It is right for mankind to build towers. We should build great structures, create beautiful art, write fascinating stories, think deep philosophies and plumb the greatest depths of truth. We should do these things, however, not for our own glory, but to the glory of our Creator and the Maker of us all. Our works should glorify God, not the self.

What we do instead is build towers to the self. We continually build towers to the self. From our business to our art, from medicine to politics, from education to entertainment, it is all about building towers to the self. We reach for our own glory, for achievements that will reach the heavens. We call it reaching for the stars, language that is eerily similar to the builders of Babel.

What we forget is that every tower built to the self will fall. That is the fate of all our towers. It doesn't matter how big, or great or vast that tower is. It doesn't matter how popular or powerful that tower is, or how much renown that tower has produced. There will come a day when that tower will fall. It will be abandoned, forgotten, then left to molder in the sands of time, collecting the dust with all the other forgotten totems of man's glory.

Take time to look at some of the plaques on the buildings of your city or the signs naming bridges after honored figures. Do you know all their names? Some have grown obscure to you for sure. Ten, thirty years ago, they were celebrated figures. What will become of their memory in another fifty years? One-hundred? A thousand? They will suffer the fate of the god-kings of Egypt who were worshiped as gods, their deeds etched in monuments that were built to last forever. Today, they are the pastime of tourists, who wander among the rocks, paying more attention to their ice cream than the monuments, unable to read the etchings of glory, and forgetting all about them as soon as they settle in for television that night.

Our towers, no matter how great, will always fall. Our towers, no matter how important they seem today, will one day be abandoned and forgotten.

The reason God stopped the building of the tower of Babel is the same reason he lets my towers, meager though they are, crumble to ruin. They are edifices of pride, nothing else. These towers to the self are an offense to God. They seek to rival his glory with the pitiful works of my hands. To take the life he has given me and use it to build towers, or try to build my name, is to squander the great gift he has laid at my feet.

In these towers we will never find what we are truly looking for. We will never find that lost confidence, that sense of belonging, that assurance that we are loved and valued by all that is important in the universe. We will never find the approval of our Father and will never find the face of our God in building monuments so great that he will take notice. That is truly what we are trying to do, make God take notice of us and give us his regard. No, we will only find that regard by forgetting ourselves and building instead for his glory.

There is another profound lesson this story teaches us. God looks down at a united humanity and sees them building a tower to the heavens. Though it is a wicked thing they do, they are at the same time displaying the unrivaled power of unity. During this time period, all people spoke the same language, and there was nothing to divide them. They were a united humanity. They were one people. When God saw what they were doing, he noticed that nothing they proposed to do was impossible if they were one, if they were united.

This is an amazing and powerful statement from the mouth of God. We should pause for a moment and consider its implications. If human beings are united, if they stand as one people, with one goal, nothing is impossible for them. Nothing is impossible. What an amazing power that is. It is a shame that such power had to be wasted, and is wasted still, in building towers to glorify the self.

This is a lesson about the incredible power of cooperation. It is one that applies to any group. It is as true for families and football teams as it is for businesses and even nations. We can also understand it as applying to the whole brotherhood of humanity. Together, in unity, much can be accomplished. With complete unity, nothing is impossible. We advance and accomplish great things through the power of cooperation.

This is significant because it is in stark contrast to what is taught in our culture. What we are taught is that advancement progresses through competition. It is through the law of rivalry, survival of the fittest, that we advance and achieve great things. Only by the gospel of self-interest does the human race advance. Competition breeds innovation, and it makes us stronger.

Essentially, we are taught rivalry. We are bred to rivalry

and raised to see each other, indeed all our fellow man, as competitors. If we do not have the strength to take hold of what is good, our rival will. If we do not hurry up and innovate, our rival will overtake us when he innovates. If we do not take all we can, there will be nothing left for us when the dust settles. Even friends, though we call them friends, are secretly rivals too. For with them we compete for esteem, for popularity, and for mates.

We are told that this gospel of self-interest and this law of competition are how human beings became great in the first place, how we became the dominant species on the planet. In fact, every species rises and evolves and advances by out-competing another species, or by growing stronger than members of its own species. Brother consumes brother, and by that feast he takes another step in the evolutionary quest. It is every man for himself in the world of nature, we are told. It is nature, brutal, merciless and self-seeking, rewarding only those who will fight harder and dirtier than his neighbor.

It is not just species, but nations and businesses that rise and fall by the same principle. Only those nations that can build better armies and learn how to destroy the best will survive. Only the company that can rise above its rivals can succeed. Only the culture that is strong enough to consume others will last long enough to write the history books. Competition, we are told, is the secret to power and advancement.

Certainly, a healthy dose of rivalry can work well. Competition can push us to excel, but competition also carries in it the seeds of destruction. For it was by competition for glory that Rome consumed herself, eaten from the inside out by warring factions and politics, more destructive than any barbarian that prowled at her borders. It is rivalry that tears families apart, dissolves the bonds of friendship, cultivates mistrust, leads us to

201

loneliness, pushes us to theft and adultery. It is rivalry that stirs up those deep feelings of alienation and unworth. It is rivalry that leads nation to war with nation, that drops bombs and launches missiles, that suits up young men to charge into machine gun fire on foreign soil with commands to kill people they do not know. It was rivalry that caused Cain to rise up and slay his brother Abel.

So rivalry and competition, though they can be a power that will help us advance, are at the same time dangerous attitudes that have consumed the human animal more than they have helped him. They are motivations that have murdered more people than every other feeling put together.

If we look through scripture, nowhere do we find that rivalry and competition are encouraged as pathways to advancement. The Bible does not teach self-interest and competition. What scripture teaches us is something radically different. Our Lord tells us, commands us, to love our neighbor as our self. Competition and rivalry may be natural, but if unchecked, they always leads to murder. This is a truth we must face if we are to ever become a humane culture—rivalry and competition unchecked will always lead to murder.

This story teaches us another root to human and cultural advancement. This story shows us there is a better way than through rivalry and competition. What we discover is that the root and power of advancement lies in cooperation. Indeed, it is in cooperation that anything can be done. For God himself acknowledges this.

I believe that if we were to study the great advances of our culture and civilization, we would find that cooperation, rather than competition, played a greater role. Even in the case of weapons being advanced in times of war, they required great cooperation to be developed and used. Perhaps, because we grow complacent, we need rivalry to inspire us. If this is so, we can find a cooperation in rivalry if we all adhere to the law of loving our neighbors as we love ourselves. But, it must be a rivalry that knows that even if we lose, then our value as human beings has not been diminished. It must realize that just because one of us has become big, it does not make me any smaller. For, this is where it grows most dangerous. The type of rivalry our world practices, the one where winning is everything, and only those who win truly matter, where the losers spend a life serving the winners—this is the deadly and murderous form of rivalry. It teaches that competition is queen of all.

This rivalry has destroyed nations, and it will destroy ours as well. Without cooperation we are doomed. But it also cannot be the forced cooperation that some would try to legislate through different systems of government. We have to be willing to give up our rivalry. We have to see and understand for ourselves the value of cooperation. We have to put aside building towers to the self and begin to work as one for the glory of God. If we were to do that, and cooperate in advancing his glory, then there is truly nothing that would be impossible for us to accomplish.

Epilogue

Genesis 12:1-3

In the Beginning

Now the Lord said to Abram, "Go from your country and your kindred and your father's house to the land that I will show you. And I will make of you a great nation, and I will bless you and make your name great, so that you will be a blessing. I will bless those who bless you, and him who dishonors you I will curse, and in you all the families of the earth shall be blessed."

Everything that has happened until this point is a prelude. A set up. These things have set the stage for the real story of the Bible. God has created the earth. He made it good. He filled it with creatures made good. He gave dominion to man that he made good. By disobedience, by the work of the serpent, sin and evil corrupted God's good work. It fell to chaos and murder. It was redeemed by the waters of the flood. But even recreated, it fell again to evil, the people building a tower to rival the power of heaven. Mankind is scattered over the face of the earth, divided in language and race.

This is where the story begins. This is where God begins again his work of redemption. Mankind is scattered, but God is planning to bring them back together.

We have just learned that nothing is impossible for man if he is united as one. I believe that this is the plan of God, to unite all mankind. United, we will then realize our potential and do great things, things we can not even imagine today. But in order to do this, we must be united under the banner of God. We must come together as his children, and as his people.

In beginning this work, God calls an old man and his wife, Abram and Sarai, and promises to make him the father of many nations. Their descendants will be more numerous than the stars of heaven or the sands of the beach, God tells him. God is starting with just one man and through that one man will create a people for himself.

This is what God has been about with us from day one, creating a people for himself. He did this when he fashioned Adam and Eve and breathed his own spirit into them. He did this when he gave the Law to Moses and set apart the Israelite nation for himself. And this is what he was about when Christ died, and his Apostles went across the world to spread the good news of the resurrected Lord. God was gathering a people for himself that would be the men and women as he made us to be.

It is not an easy task, making a people for God. For one, we must be a good people, fearing God and obeying his commands, loving him and loving one another. But in order for this to be truly accomplished, we must also be free. Without that freedom we can't really be good people. Without that freedom we can't really love. What God calls us to be is both free and good. Not an easy proposition.

If we are to be truly free and good, God cannot wave a miracle wand and make us so. For this plan to work, we have to choose to be good. And we have to choose to be free. We have to choose the dove over the serpent. We have to decide to trust in God's ways over our own. To do this is to find true freedom.

The serpent is bondage and always has been. He has successfully portrayed himself as the fun option, as the free option. To follow the serpent looks like having a good time, doing what you want. If nothing else, we must admit that the propaganda machine for evil is much more effective than the one for good. But it doesn't change the truth that evil is bondage, not freedom, no matter how it presents itself.

What is true and good does not need to campaign for itself. True virtue stands on its own. It doesn't need to entice man with pleasure or power or wealth. Virtue, like truth, is self-justifying. You know it is right because it is right. It stands for life and hope and goodness. If we cannot see these things as true and right, then we are not ready to live as free people.

This is what God is working for as much as he is working for our virtue. God wants us to be free people. Over and again throughout scripture, we hear the promise of freedom. Freedom was granted to the Hebrew people, delivered out of slavery. Paul discusses the work of Jesus as the work of freedom. And Christ himself promised that if we abide in him, the truth, then that truth will set us free.

The greatest bondage we experience in life is not political or economic, it is spiritual. Evil and sin have chained us in fetters stronger than any that can be forged here on earth. Sin can bind the will as surely as it can deceive and blind the mind. Our ability to act as free will people is inhibited as long as we submit to the serpent in us. As long as we choose evil over good, lies over truth, we are choosing slavery over freedom.

Despite what the propagandists for evil might say, to engage in sin is not freedom but bondage. To allow the serpent to make our decisions is to give up our freedom and to allow sin to make decisions for us. Freedom is found when we live by the dove, by the voice and word of God.

The work of Christ is a work of liberation. As we exist now, we are held captive by the serpent, guided by our pride, selfishness, rivalry, and vanity. We are not able to make our own choices. Rather, we are compelled to act as our evil nature commands us.

As long as we rely upon our own insight over the word of God, we will remain in bondage to the serpent. This is a hard truth to accept, to lean on God's ways and word over our own understanding. But this is a truth that can set us free.

Because truth is what sets us free, to begin to accept truth is to begin to accept freedom in your life again. As we become free, as the serpent loses his dominion over our lives, we become free to be the people that God made. We are free to live in the image of God that we bear within. We are free to be alive.

This is the great work of God in us, the work of life. In our few and fleeting days, we are presented with an opportunity, one that we can only take hold of if we are living our lives in the freedom of God. To be alive is to be free.

Life is not what many will mistake it for today. Being alive is not a biological state. Life is not active cells, and blood flow, and brain activity. These things are a part of life, but they are not life.

To truly be alive is to reflect and live in the image of God. We each have that image in us. In all of us is that capacity, not to be God, but to reflect the glory of God. We can imitate God but with the knowledge that we will never be God.

This is not a deficiency of any sort, or a weakness. This is simply who we are made to be. We were made to reflect his nature and cultivate the image of God within us. To do so is to be alive.

Today, there is a great error about how we find life, or how we truly live. Conventional wisdom tells us that to take is the key to a full and meaningful life. We must take wealth, or experience. We must do grand things. We must live an epic life, something to make others jealous, something that others will talk about long after we are gone. We must travel to exotic places, party with powerful people, and experience all the luxury and pleasure that life offers. We must take from life all that we can get out of it.

But our God is not one who takes. He is one who gives. He gave us this universe. He gave us life. He gave us his image upon our souls. He gave us his only son. If we are to strive to imitate God, we would be givers too. We would not live to see how much we could take out of life but how much we can give back to it.

To imitate God, to live in his image, is to pour of ourselves into life. All the gifts he has given us, we give them back. To make the world friendlier, more lovely, more beautiful, abundant, more meaningful—this is how we give to life. Teach, love, grow, reach out, be a friend— this is how we live. We are called to offer what we have, what we are, for the benefit of mankind. Unlike today's world—which preaches to greedily withhold, work for your profit, take all you can from life, to be mere consumers of life—God calls us to give, to serve, to contribute, and to take care of others.

We should not live as consumers but as givers of life. To be a consumer is to act out of hunger. To be a giver is to act out of abundance. To give of life is to discover the secret of the meaning of life, and then discover that it is no secret at all. It is a secret open and available to any who would be free, and who would live as God made us.

It is an often overlooked fact in the story of Abraham that he will never live to see the covenant fulfilled. God promises to make Abraham the father of a great nation, to be a name through which all the nations will be blessed. But Abraham will never see this happen. He will die as a man with only one son. He will not see the descendants line up before him, as countless as the stars. When he leaves the earth, he will only have a promise of the future.

There is a lesson here if we would understand and live by it, that is guaranteed to make the world a better place. All that Abraham did was not for his present benefit. For sure, he was blessed with abundance, but that was not the blessing God promised. What Abraham was promised, and what he labored for, was a blessing that would not come to realization until a distant time in the future. He worked for something that he would not see. Abraham worked for the good, not of today, but of tomorrow.

This is a lesson that is sorely forgotten today, to work for the benefit of tomorrow. We work for the benefit of today. We want to enjoy the fruits of our labor, and we want them now. To work for something we will never see is considered stupid and pointless. To work, and have someone else enjoy, is to be a sucker and to waste the little time we have here on earth. We live for the present, to enjoy and live for the now.

This philosophy has so overtaken us that we have come to threaten the future. Far from being like Abraham, who worked for the good of the future, we live for today so much that we have all but guaranteed a grimmer future. The economic policies of our nation have promised to throw our grandchildren into debt. We toy around with technologies without any regard for the long term effect on our world. We build up cheap and inexpensive houses that will not last past our own lifetimes. We would rather pacify our children today with media instead of taking the hard road of teaching them discipline, raising them to be happy today rather than be strong tomorrow. We have even threatened the environment of tomorrow, so that we might live an easier and more abundant life today.

All of God's promises, we find, are promises of the future. They are to be realized at some distant time, some further time, some time, likely, we will not be alive to see. To work for the cause of life is to work for the benefit of tomorrow.

If we were all to work for the benefit, the real benefit of future generations, then we would not fail to build a better world. This is true of the individual life as well as the collective life. If you work for your future, personally, it will most likely be a good one. Even tomorrow, when you are working for another tomorrow, you will inevitably reap the benefits of your work done today. For what we enjoy today was work that was done yesterday. And what we will enjoy tomorrow is work done today.

This is the way life has always been. To enjoy life we must be far-seeing, we must be people willing to work for the future. To work and live for today is to doom tomorrow. But to work for tomorrow is to open wide the gates of the future.

The true work we are called to in life is not a work for our present enjoyment. It is not even a work for our future enjoyment. The true work we are called to in life is to work for the benefit of future generations. We are to work for a yield we will never see and experience.

Dr. Elton Trueblood once said, "A man has made at least a start on discovering the meaning of human life when he plants shade trees under which he knows full well he will never sit."

This is a strange sentiment to us, we who have been raised to work for ourselves alone. It is strange, and perhaps frightening, to even think that we should work for the benefit of the future, to work for a benefit we will never enjoy. But this is where we will find the secret of life and the true joy of living. This is where we will discover purpose and meaning. This is where we will feel confident that we are cultivating the image of God in us, because we are cultivating it in our world.

In all we do, we should always consider the effect our actions will have on future generations. We should ask ourselves, will this in any way bring harm to the children of tomorrow? To take it even further, we should ask what benefit our contributions will have on future generations, in what way will this help the people of tomorrow?

In order to be able to live and act this way, we must have hope. It is no surprise that as we work less and less for the future, and more for our present enjoyment and benefit, we are a less hopeful people. We are beginning not to look forward to tomorrow, but to dread what tomorrow may bring. We are beginning to live lives not of hope, but despair.

This does not have to be. We can be people of hope again, people of the future. There is no reason not to look forward to tomorrow, for we are the builders of tomorrow. In order to build it well, and to build it right, we must build it as men and women made in the image of God. We must accept that we were made in his image, made as human beings, and that is always what we will be. We are not gods, nor were we meant to be gods.

To accept our humanity is to begin to make the most of what it means to be human. Being human is not only something we should accept, it is something we should rejoice in, something we celebrate. All of us were chosen to be made, chosen to reflect the glory and image of God. All of us were chosen to be alive, to be a part and manifestation of life. This is reason not only to celebrate, but to hope.

When God promised to make Abraham the father of a great nation, he also promised that through him all nations would be blessed. Abraham trusted and believed. Out of him came the patriarchs, Isaac, Jacob, and Joseph. Out of him came Moses, who led his people out of slavery and received the Law from God. Out of him came the nation of Israel, the kings and prophets and people of God. And ultimately, from him came Jesus Christ, who would bear the sins of the world upon his back, conquer sin and death, rise again to new life, and open the gates of paradise for us that we could always live in hope.

It all began with a promise to an old man who believed enough to hope in the future. Much of what is good in our world can be traced back to that one man who believed in that one promise. Indeed, everything that is good in our world comes from some person believing in the promise of tomorrow. If we are truly to make a better world, if we are truly to find meaning and purpose and passion in life, it will also come from our efforts to build a better world tomorrow instead of trying to take all that we can from the world today.

To do this, we must trust not in the serpent, but the dove. We must surely cultivate our intellect, educate our minds, and learn as much as we can about ourselves and this vast and beautiful universe that we live in. More importantly, though, we must cultivate the dove within us—the faith that leans not upon its own understanding, but upon the wisdom and word of God. Only in trusting in the dove over the serpent will we understand what is good and true and become people capable of living lives that are good and true.

As human beings—made in the image of God and animated with his own breath—we have been given a special place in his creation. We were made stewards of the earth, keepers of the garden, given dominion over all the other creatures with whom we share the earth. More importantly, we were made as the builders of tomorrow. If we have no hope in tomorrow, it is because we have no hope in the future that we are building today. And as long as we try to shape the world into our own image, as long as we live to take from life, as long as we trust in the serpent instead of the dove, we will always be in desperate search of that hope. If we would be people of hope, if we would be people who look forward to tomorrow, it will come from believing and trusting in God—in the great work of life that he has begun in the universe, and in the faith that tomorrow life will be good again.

To God be all the glory forever and ever, Amen.

Acknowledgements

I would like to extend a special thanks to everyone who helped make this book possible. I would especially like to thank Tom Moore for his patient feedback that gave me the idea in the first place. Julius and Tony for their work on making it all happen. Harris Murray and her priceless help in editing. And of course, my wife, Elizabeth Cely, who has proven an invaluable partner in life.